Mark Sarnecki

Elementary Music Rudiments

Library and Archives Canada Cataloguing in Publication

Sarnecki, Mark, 1959-
    Elementary music rudiments / Mark Sarnecki.

ISBN-13: 978-1-55440-075-1 (basic)
ISBN-13: 978-1-55440-076-8 (intermediate)
ISBN-13: 978-1-55440-077-5 (advanced)
ISBN-10: 1-55440-076-7 (intermediate)

1. Music theory--Elementary works. I. Title.

MT7.S2467 2006   781   C2006-904353-1

© Copyright 2001 The Frederick Harris Music Co., Limited
All Rights Reserved

ISBN 978-1-55440-076-8

Preface

The study of theory is an important part of a complete musical education. Familiarity with the basic concepts of music theory aids in musical literacy, including notation, sight reading, ear training, and memory.

The *Elementary Music Rudiments* series is a comprehensive course covering notation, pitch, rhythm, meter, key signatures, major and minor scales, intervals, chords, modal scales, melody writing, the keyboard, and beginning harmony.

This book is designed to be used in a number of ways including self-study, one-on-one music teaching, and as a text for group study in the classroom. It is suitable for use by all instrumentalists and vocalists. The information is presented in a clear, concise, and systematic manner, and the easy to understand workbook format offers the student plenty of exercises to practice and master the concepts of music rudiments.

Mark Sarnecki

The title of each level in the *Elementary Music Rudiments* series is changing to more accurately describe its content. The following titles are used interchangeably throughout the *Elementary Music Rudiments* series:

Basic Rudiments *is equivalent to...*   Preliminary Rudiments

Intermediate Rudiments *is equivalent to...*   Grade One Rudiments

Advanced Rudiments *is equivalent to...*   Grade Two Rudiments

CONTENTS

PRELIMINARY REVIEW

SCALES

The Major Scale

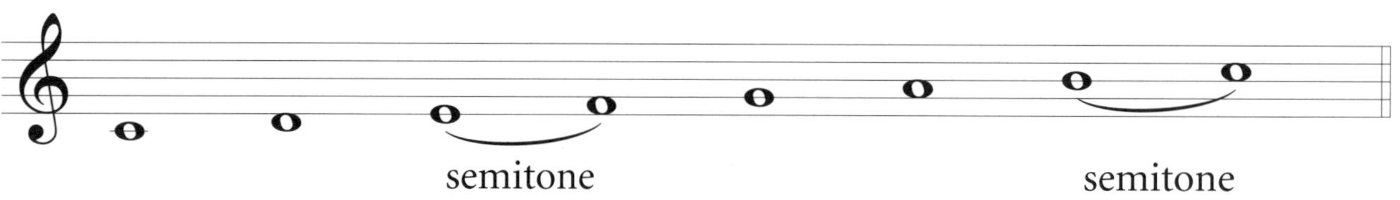

In a major scale, semitones occur between scale degrees *three and four,* and *seven and eight.*

The Natural Minor Scale

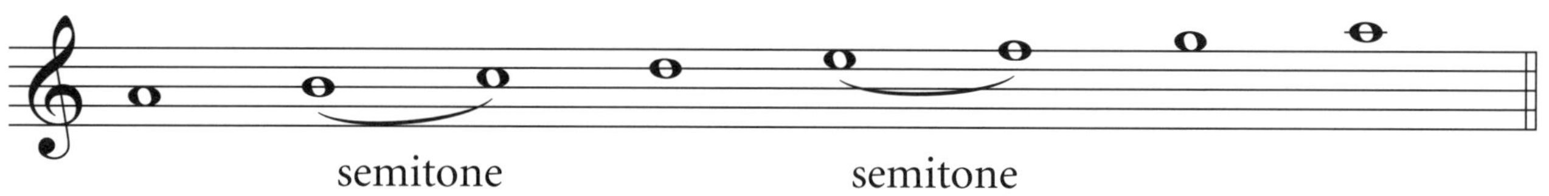

In a natural minor scale, semitones occur between scale degrees *two and three,* and *five and six.*

The Harmonic Minor Scale

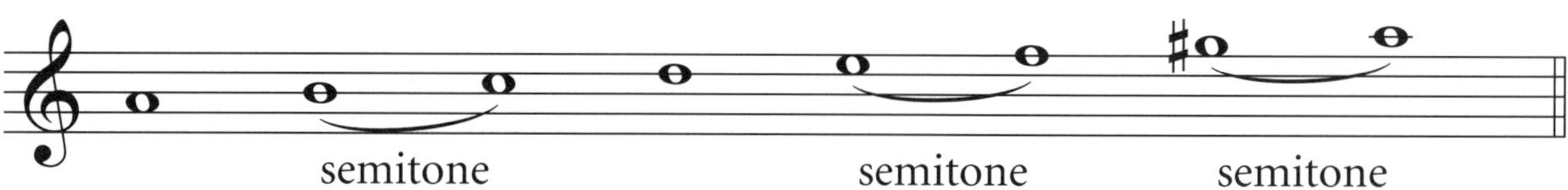

In a harmonic minor scale, semitones occur between scale degrees *two and three, five and six,* and *seven and eight.*

The Melodic Minor Scale

In a melodic minor scale, semitones occur between scale degrees *two and three,* and *seven and eight* ascending; and between scale degrees *six and five,* and *three and two,* descending.

KEY SIGNATURES

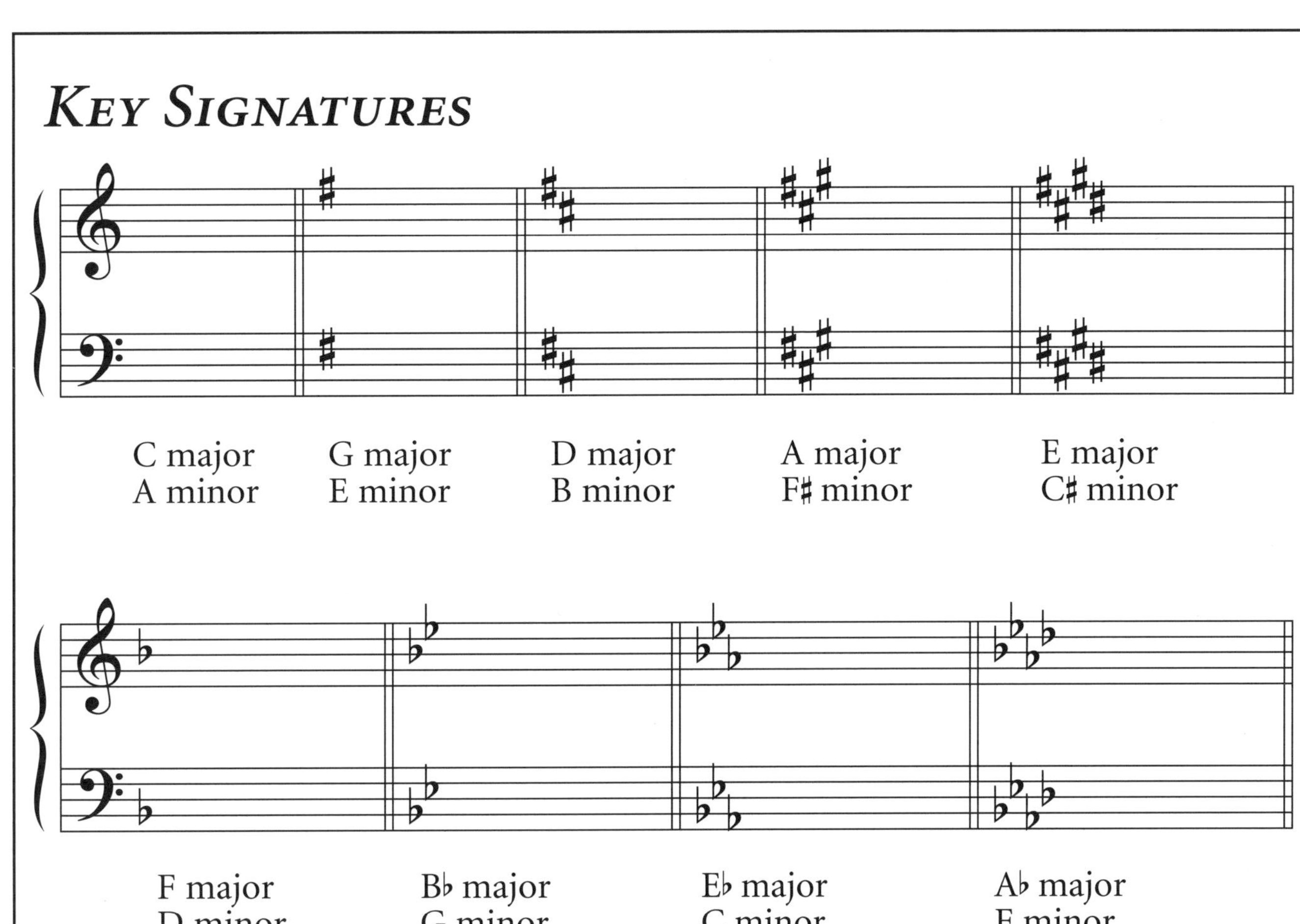

INTERVALS

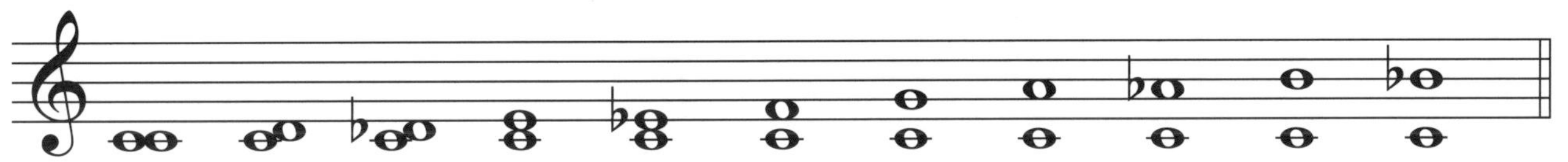

DEGREES OF THE SCALE

I	Tonic
IV	Subdominant
V	Dominant

Triads

Simple Time

PRELIMINARY ITALIAN TERMS AND SIGNS

a tempo	return to the previous tempo
adagio	a slow tempo (between *andante* and *largo*)
allegretto	fairly fast (a little slower than *allegro*)
allegro	fast
andante	moderately slowly; at a walking pace
andantino	a little faster than *andante*
cantabile	in a singing style
crescendo, cresc.	becoming louder
da capo, D.C.	from the beginning
decrescendo, decresc.	becoming softer
diminuendo, dim.	becoming softer
dolce	sweet
fermata 𝄐	pause; hold note or rest longer than written value
fine	the end
forte, **𝆑**	loud
fortissimo, **𝆑𝆑**	very loud
grazioso	graceful
larghetto	not as slow as *largo*
largo	very slow and broad
legato	smoothly
lento	slow
maestoso	majestic
mano destra, M.D.	right hand
mano sinistra, M.S.	left hand
marcato	marked or stressed
mezzo forte, **m𝆑**	moderately loud
mezzo piano, **mp**	moderately soft
moderato	at a moderate tempo
ottava, 8va	the interval of an octave
piano, **p**	soft
pianissimo, **pp**	very soft
presto	very fast
prestissimo	as fast as possible
rallentando, rall.	slowing down
ritardando, rit.	slowing down gradually
staccato	sharply detached
tempo	speed at which music is performed
Tempo primo, Tempo I	return to the original tempo

SIGNS

accent: a stressed note

tie: hold for the combined value of the tied notes

slur: play the notes *legato*

repeat signs: repeat the music within the double bars

staccato: play the notes sharply detached

fermata: a pause; hold the note or rest longer than its written value

pedale: with pedal

ottava: play one octave above the written pitch

dal segno, (D.S.): from the sign

crescendo: becoming louder

decrescendo: becoming softer

ACCIDENTALS

<table>
<tr><td>✖</td><td>The double sharp sign raises a natural note one whole tone (two semitones), or raises a note that is sharp one semitone.</td></tr>
<tr><td>𝄫</td><td>The double flat lowers a natural note one whole tone (two semitones), or lowers a flattened note one semitone.</td></tr>
</table>

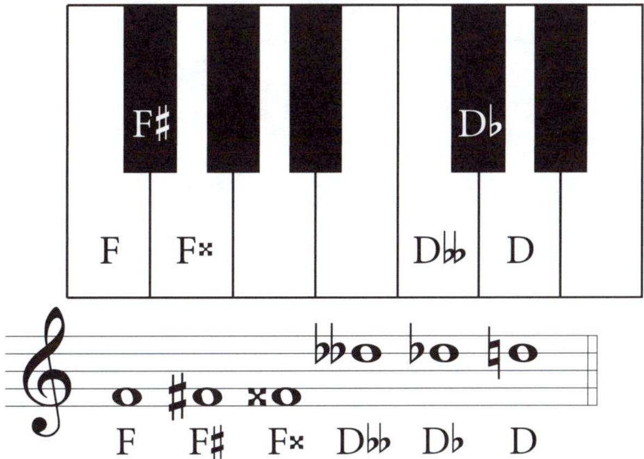

Every note, with the exception of G sharp/A flat, can have three names.

A semitone that consists of two notes with the same letter name is called a *chromatic semitone*.

A semitone that consists of two notes with different letter names is called a *diatonic semitone.*

A *whole tone* is made up of two semitones. Whole tones usually have two different letter names in alphabetical order. For example, C to D, A flat to B flat, and F double sharp to G double sharp are all whole tones.

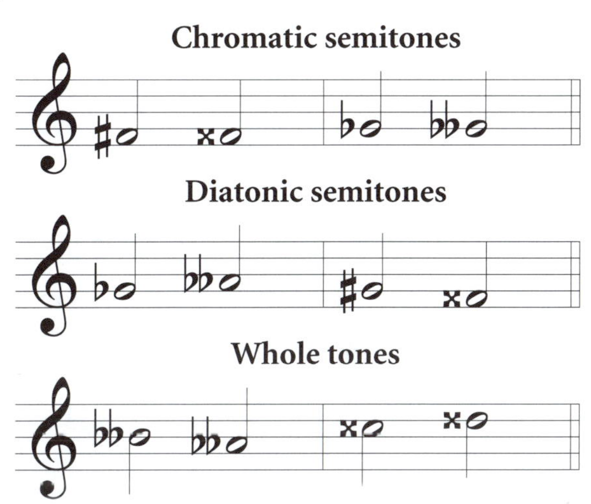

1. Write chromatic semitones above the following notes.

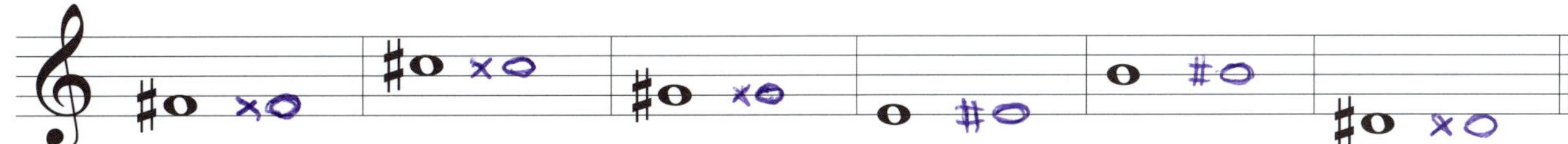

2. Write diatonic semitones above the following notes.

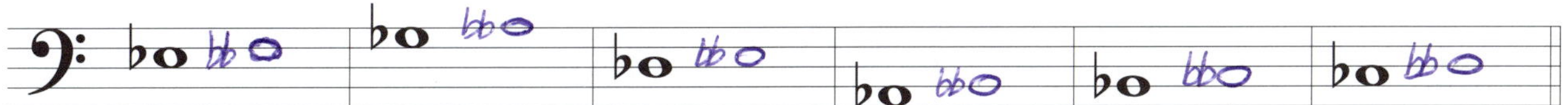

3. Write whole tones above the following notes.

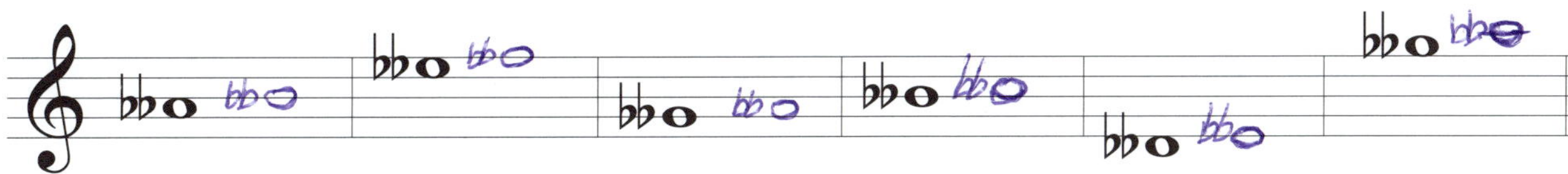

4. Write chromatic semitones below the following notes.

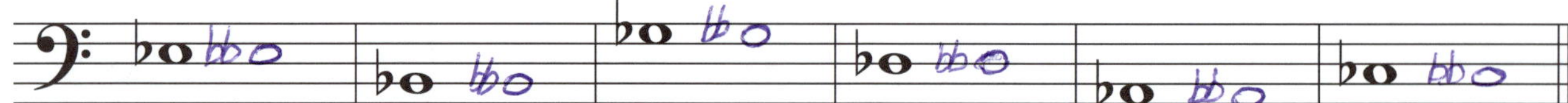

5. Write diatonic semitones below the following notes.

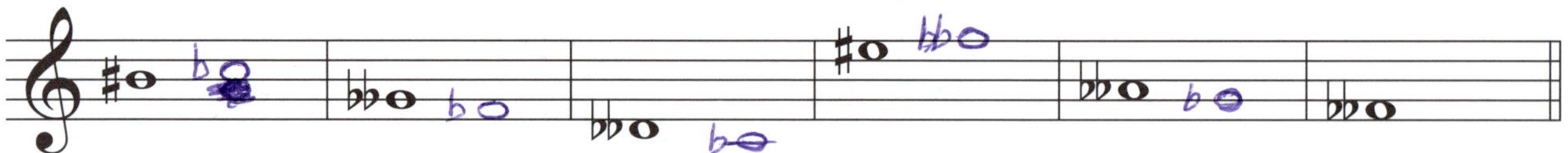

6. Write whole tones below the following notes.

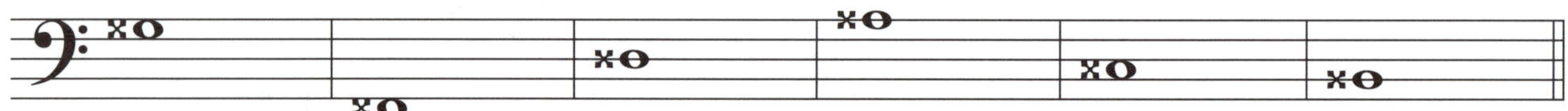

DEGREES OF THE SCALE

Every note or degree of a scale has a specific title. Here is a list of the names for the degrees of the scale:

I	Tonic
II	Supertonic
III	Mediant
IV	Subdominant
V	Dominant
VI	Submediant
VII	Leading Tone
VIII	Tonic (I)

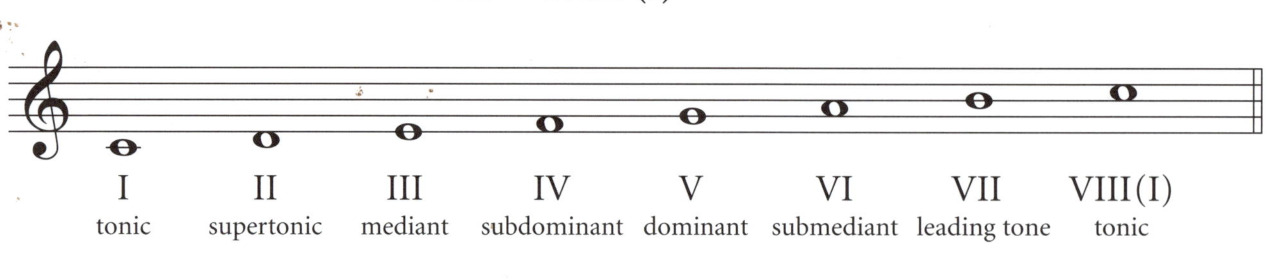

MAJOR SCALES

THE CIRCLE OF FIFTHS

The **circle of fifths** relates keys by 5ths. We start with a circle divided into twelve sections, like a clock, with C in the "12" position.

The sharp keys are set to the right (moving clockwise) in order of the number of sharps in their key signatures.

The flat keys are set to the left (moving counterclockwise) in order of the number of flats in their key signatures.

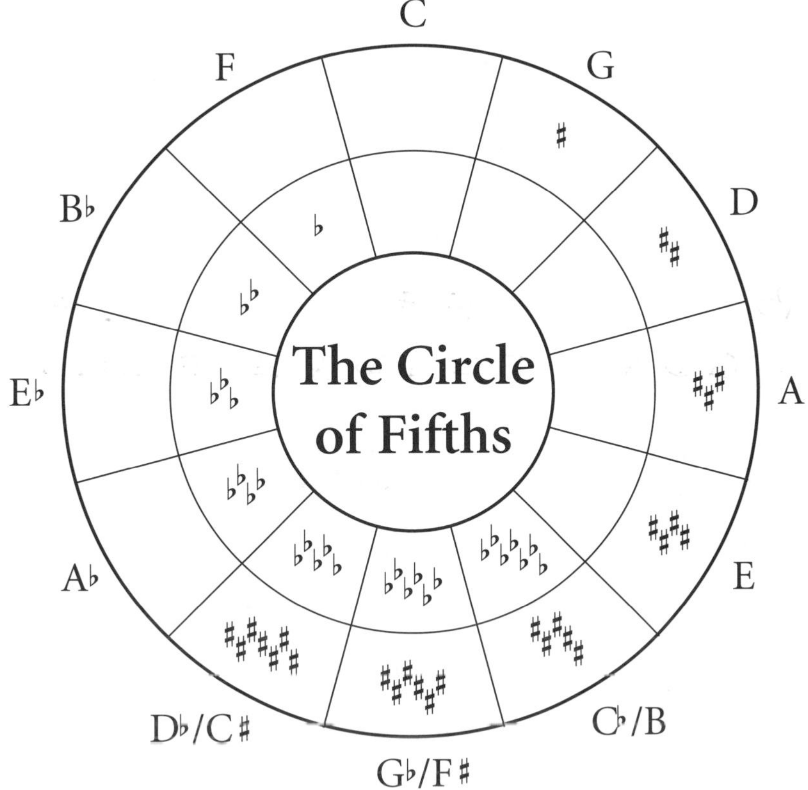

The arrangement of keys shows two things:

1. The distance between each key and the next is a 5th.

2. Three pairs of keys share the same spots in the circle:

    D flat/C sharp, G flat/F sharp, and C flat/B.

    These three pairs of keys are **enharmonic** — they have the same pitch but the notes are named differently.

Here is the order of sharps in a key signature: F C G D A E B

Here is the order of flats in a key signature: B E A D G C F

MAJOR SCALES

Sharps and flats are grouped in a specific order when they are placed on the staff. The following exercise shows the order of sharps as they appear on the staff.

1. Name the major key and write the sharps represented by each key signature below.

The following exercise shows the order of flats as they appear on the staff.

2. Name the major key and write the flats represented by each key signature below.

3. Write the following notes and key signatures on the grand staves below.

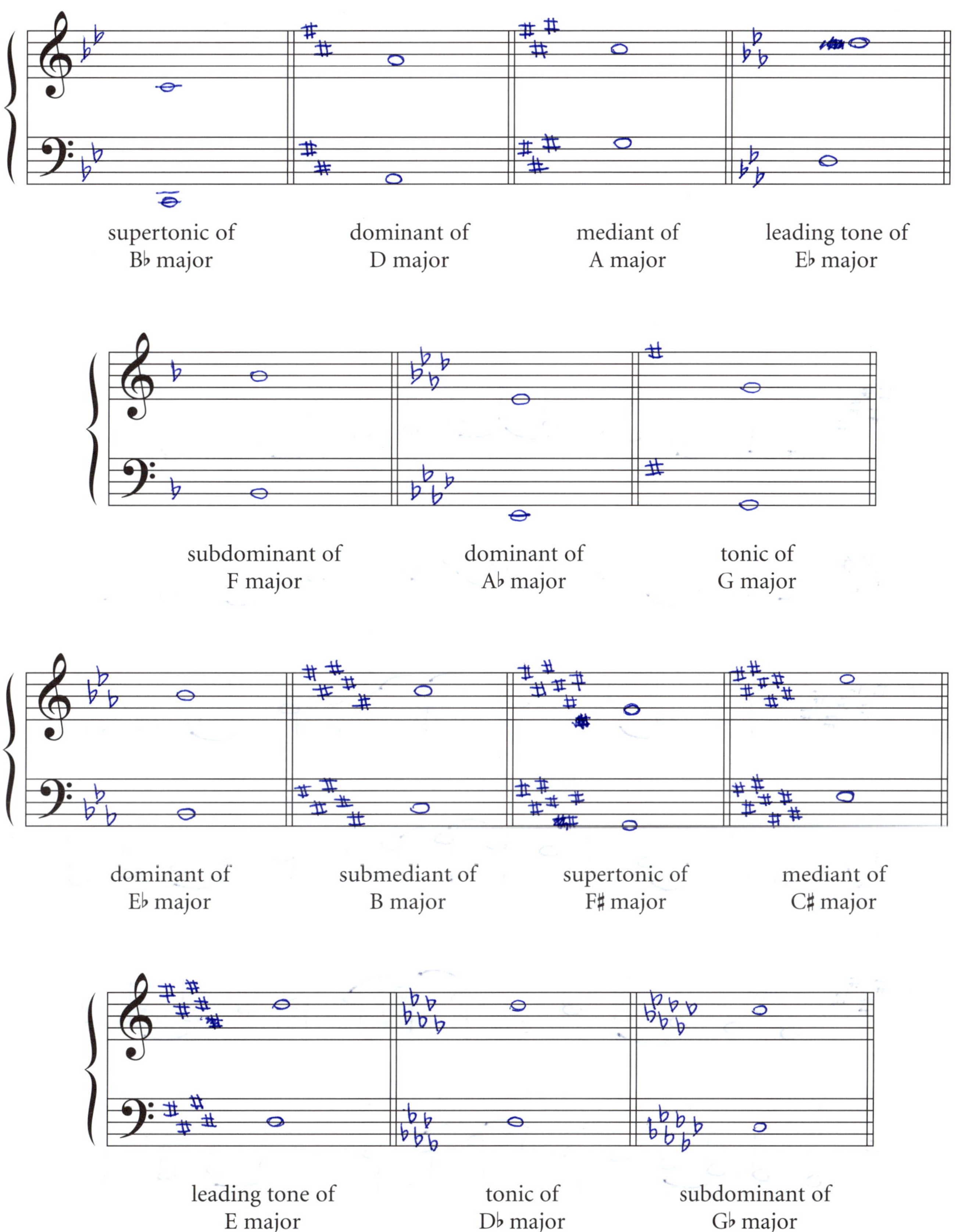

MAJOR SCALES

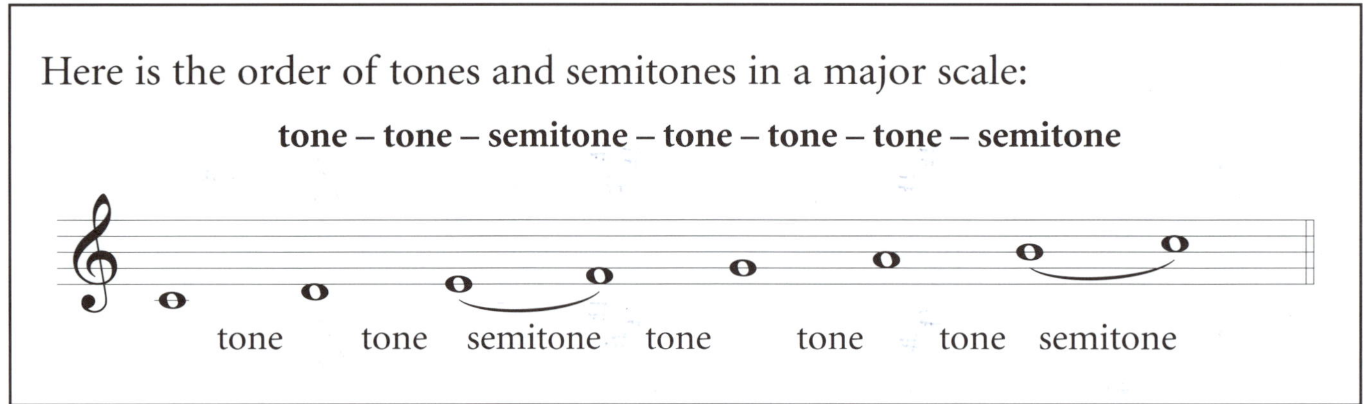

Here is the order of tones and semitones in a major scale:

tone – tone – semitone – tone – tone – tone – semitone

1. Write the following scales in half notes, ascending and descending, using key signatures. Mark the semitones with a slur.

B major

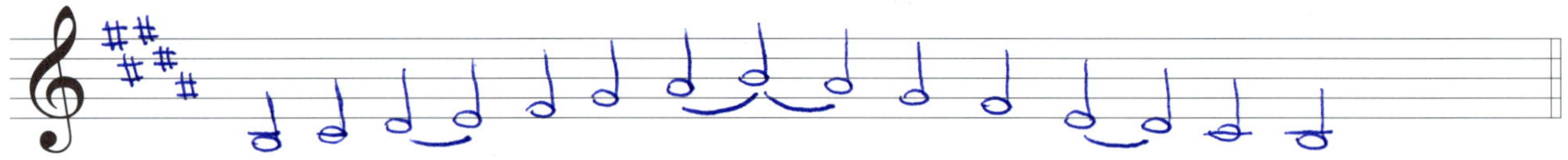

Eb major

F# major

Ab major

E major

G major

2. Write the following scales in quarter notes, ascending and descending, using accidentals instead of a key signature. Mark the semitones with a slur.

3. Write the following scales in whole notes, ascending and descending, using a key signature.

The major scale with C♯ as the dominant

The major scale with a key signature of six flats

The major scale with B♭ as the leading tone

The major scale with a key signature of two sharps

The major scale with F as the supertonic

The major scale with a key signature of three sharps

The major scale with F as the mediant

The major scale with D♭ as the subdominant

4. For the following key signatures, name the major key and identify the degree of the scale for the given notes.

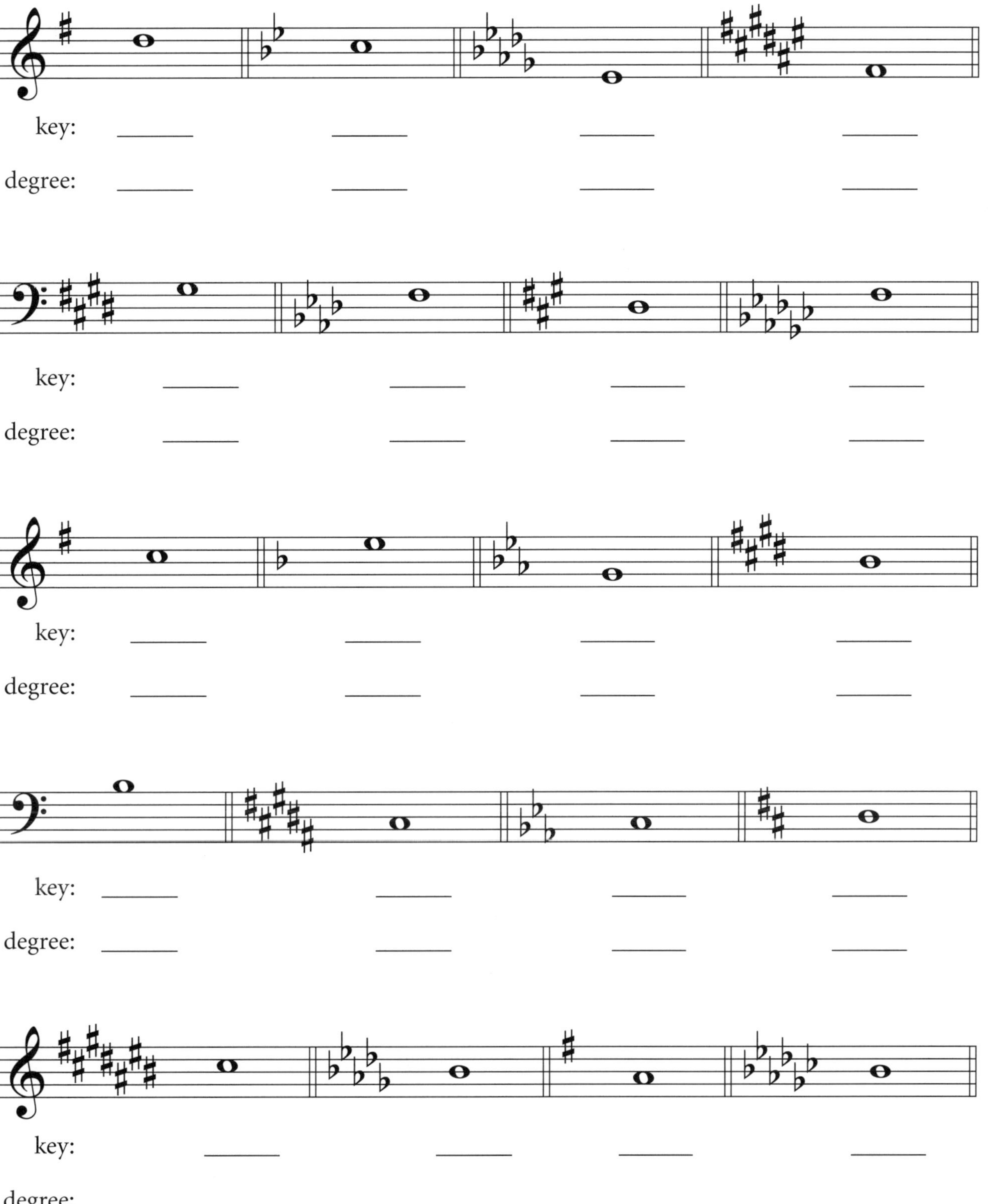

key: _______   _______   _______   _______

degree: _______   _______   _______   _______

key: _______   _______   _______   _______

degree: _______   _______   _______   _______

key: _______   _______   _______   _______

degree: _______   _______   _______   _______

key: _______   _______   _______   _______

degree: _______   _______   _______   _______

key: _______   _______   _______   _______

degree: _______   _______   _______   _______

MINOR SCALES

For each major scale, there is a **relative minor key**. Major and minor keys that are related use the same key signature. The relative minor of a major key is three semitones *lower*.

RELATIVE MAJOR AND MINOR KEYS

Major Keys	Sharps and Flats	Minor Keys
C	—	A
G	F♯	E
D	F♯, C♯	B
A	F♯, C♯, G♯	F♯
E	F♯, C♯, G♯, D♯	C♯
B	F♯, C♯, G♯, D♯, A♯	G♯
F♯	F♯, C♯, G♯, D♯, A♯, E♯	D♯
C♯	F♯, C♯, G♯, D♯, A♯, E♯, B♯	A♯
F	B♭	D
B♭	B♭, E♭	G
E♭	B♭, E♭, A♭	C
A♭	B♭, E♭, A♭, D♭	F
D♭	B♭, E♭, A♭, D♭, G♭	B♭
G♭	B♭, E♭, A♭, D♭, G♭, C♭	E♭

A major scale and a minor scale that have the same tonic are called *tonic major* and *tonic minor*. For example, F major is the tonic major of F minor — and F minor is the tonic minor of F major.

When a minor scale is written with no accidentals, it is called a **natural minor scale**.

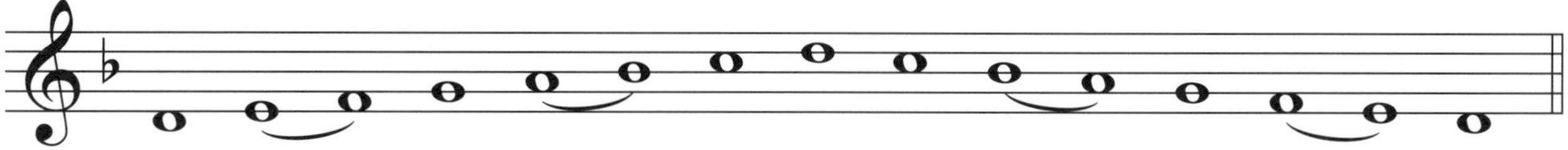

D natural minor

In a natural minor scale, there are semitones between notes *two* and *three*, and notes *five* and *six*.

The **harmonic minor scale** is formed by raising the seventh degree of the natural minor scale.

D harmonic minor

In a harmonic minor scale, there are semitones between notes *two* and *three, five* and *six,* and *seven* and *eight.*

The **melodic minor scale** is formed by raising the sixth and seventh degrees of the natural minor scale ascending, and lowering the sixth and seventh degrees descending.

D melodic minor

In a melodic minor scale, semitones occur between notes *two* and *three,* and *seven* and *eight* ascending, and between notes *six* and *five,* and *three* and *two* descending.

1. Name the key and the type (natural, harmonic, melodic) of the following minor scales.

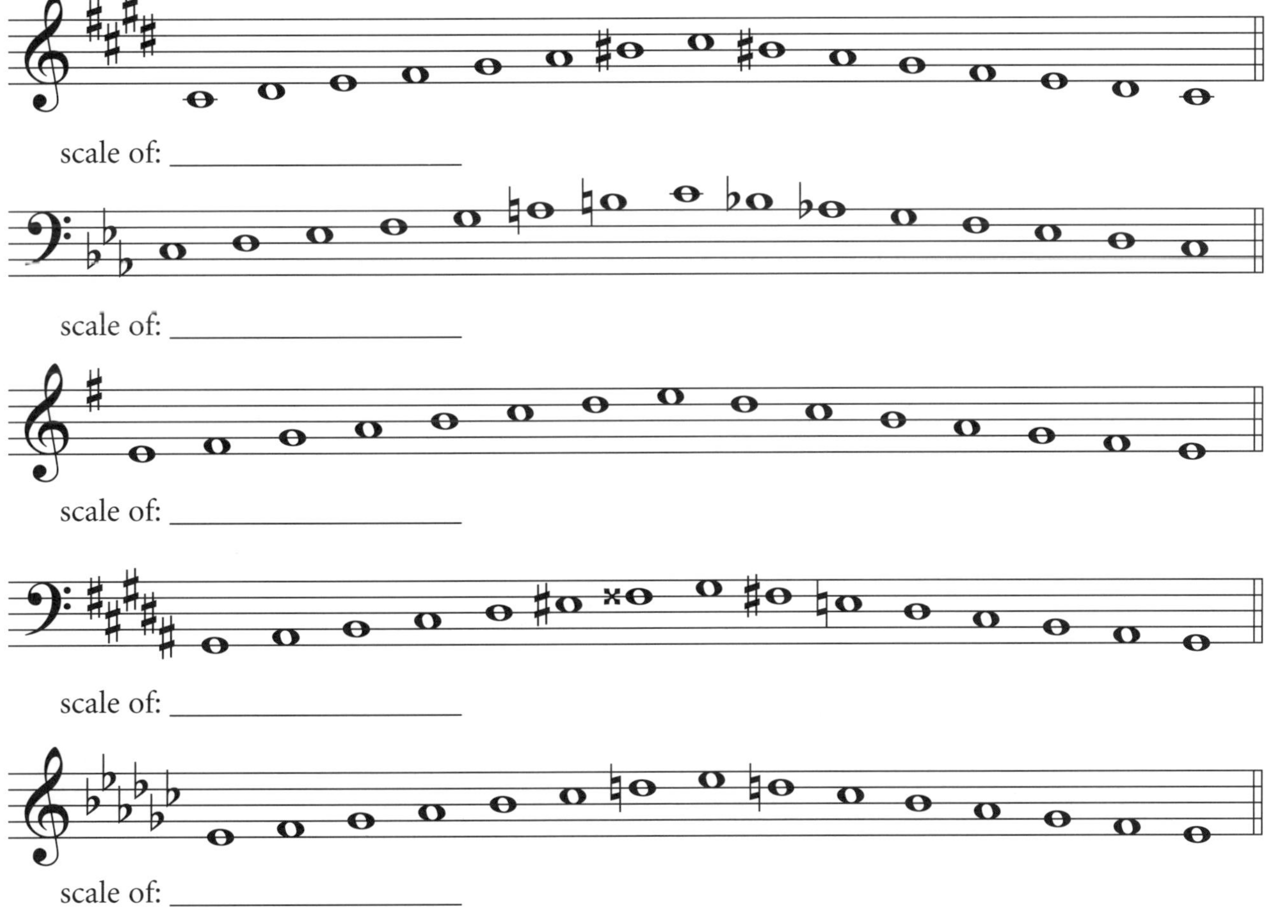

scale of: _________________

scale of: _________________

scale of: _________________

scale of: _________________

scale of: _________________

2. Write the following scales, ascending and descending, using key signatures.

D harmonic minor in half notes

C♯ melodic minor in eighth notes

F natural minor in quarter notes

E melodic minor in whole notes

F♯ harmonic minor in sixteenth notes

C melodic minor in dotted half notes

G♯ harmonic minor in sixteenth notes

E♭ natural minor in whole notes

B melodic minor in dotted quarter notes

B♭ harmonic minor in eighth notes

3. Name the minor keys for the following key signatures.

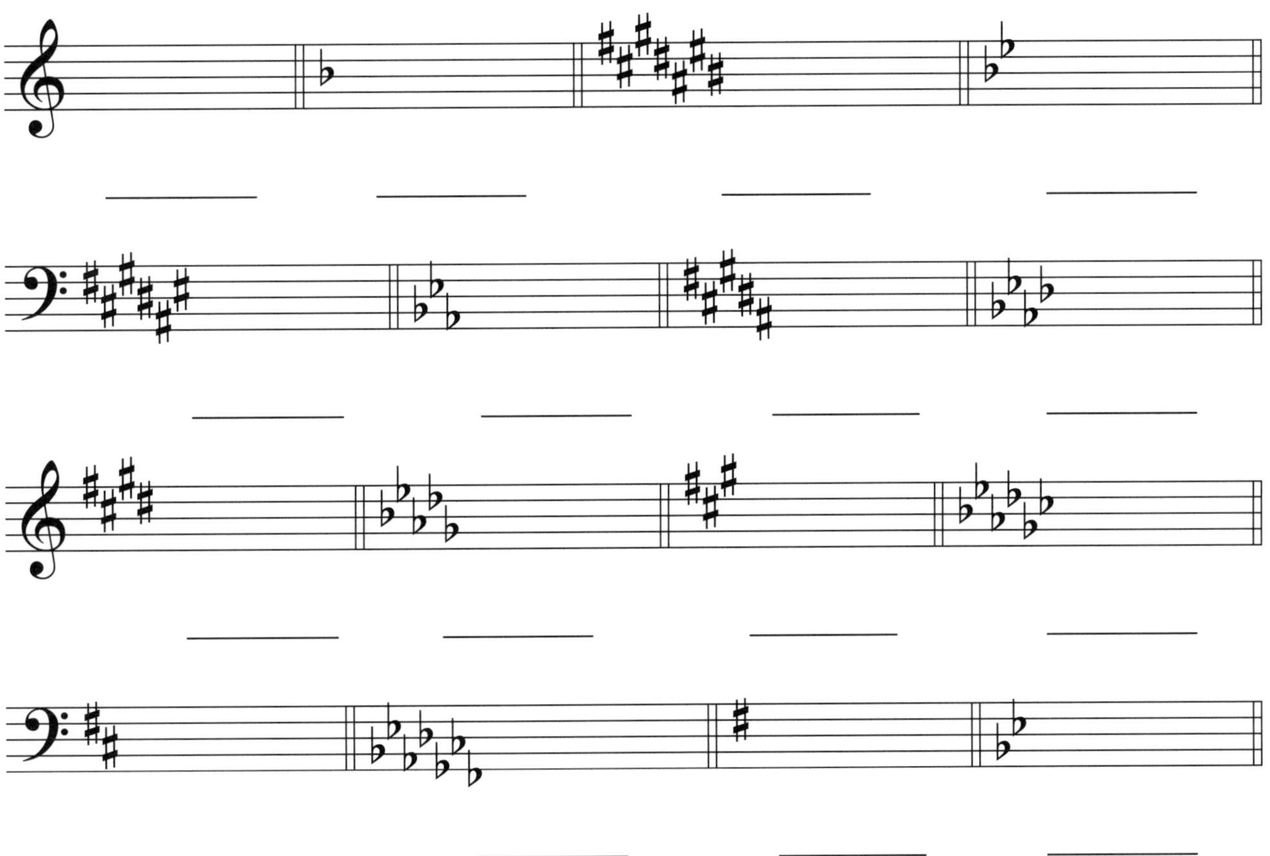

4. Name the relative minors of the following major keys.

F♯ major _____________   B♭ major _____________

G major _____________   E♭ major _____________

C♯ major _____________   E major _____________

A♭ major _____________   D♭ major _____________

C major _____________   F major _____________

B major _____________   G♭ major _____________

A major _____________   C♭ major _____________

D major _____________

5.   Write the following scales, ascending and descending, using the correct key signature.

A major

The relative melodic minor of A major

The tonic harmonic minor of A major

F♯ major from dominant to dominant

E♭ major from supertonic to supertonic

G harmonic minor from leading note to leading note

B♭ melodic minor

The tonic major of B♭ minor

The relative harmonic minor of C♯ major from mediant to mediant

B major from subdominant to subdominant

6. Write the following scales, ascending and descending, using accidentals instead of a key signature.

The relative minor, harmonic form, of D♭ major

The tonic minor, melodic form, of C major

F♯ natural minor from submediant to submediant

B harmonic minor from tonic to tonic

The melodic minor with G♯ as the dominant

The natural minor with E as the supertonic

G♭ major from mediant to mediant

C♯ major

The major scale with D♯ as the submediant

The major scale with G♯ as the leading tone

7. Add clefs, key signatures and any necessary accidentals to form the following scales.

F harmonic minor

Db major

Eb melodic minor

C# natural minor

B major

G# harmonic minor

8. Learn the following Italian terms and definitions.

animato	lively, animated
brillante	brilliant
con	with
con brio	with vigour, spirit
con espressione	with expression
espressivo	expressive, with expression
leggiero	light, nimble, quick
tranquillo	quiet, tranquil

CHROMATIC SCALES

Major and Minor scales are **diatonic**. They are made up of tones and semitones, and contain only notes that belong to the scale.

A **chromatic scale** is made up of only semitones and contains all twelve notes in the octave. There are two types of chromatic scales: the chromatic scale that has no key signature, and the chromatic scale that is based on a key.

There are two simple rules for chromatic scales.

1. Never use the same letter name more than twice.
2. Do not change the name of the tonic note enharmonically.

Chromatic Scales Without a Key Signature

In this chromatic scale without a key signature, the notes are *raised going up* and *lowered going down*. When you write this type of scale, you use sharps as soon as possible on the way up, and flats as soon as possible on the way down.

Here is a chromatic scale starting on C. Sharps are used on the way up and flats are used on the way down. *Notice that the bar line in the middle cancels all the accidentals used on the way up.*

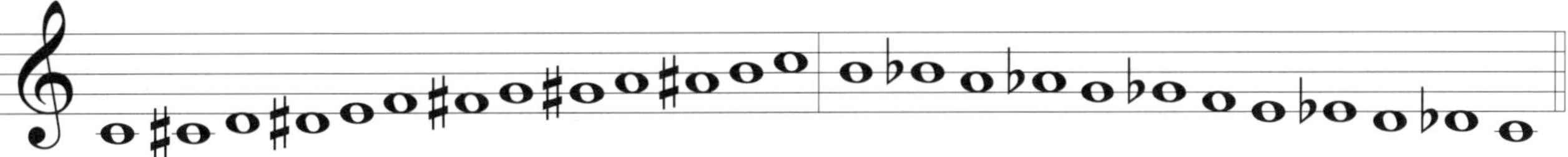

Here is a chromatic scale starting on D flat. This scale must begin with flats but it changes to sharps as soon as possible on the way up. Flats are used all the way down.

1. Write the following scales, ascending and descending.

Chromatic scale starting on E

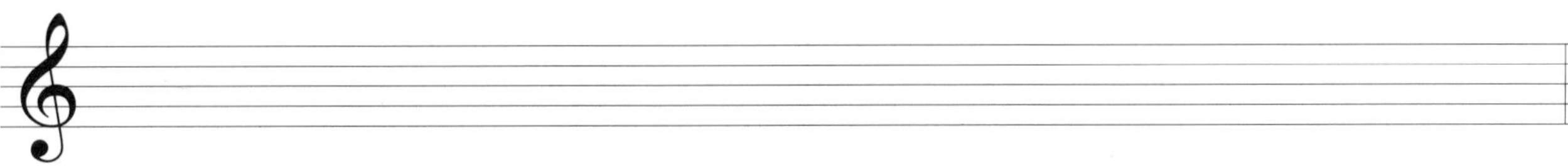

Chromatic scale starting on F♯

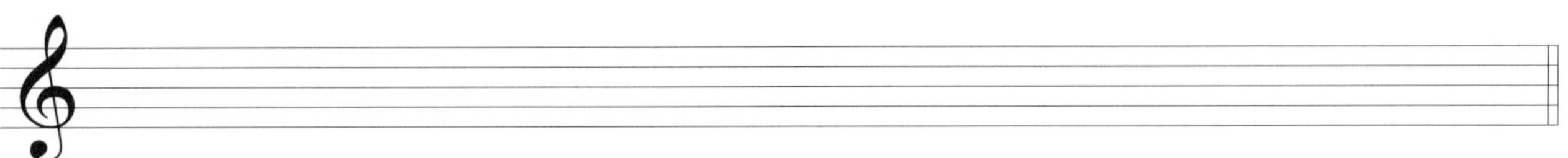

CHROMATIC SCALES

Chromatic Scales Based on a Key

A chromatic scale may also be based on a major scale. This form of chromatic scale may be written with or without a key signature.

To write this type of chromatic scale without a key signature, follow these three steps:

1. Determine the tonic and dominant notes by using the first note as the tonic of a major scale. Write the tonic and dominant notes, ascending and descending.

    In the example below, the scale begins on E. The tonic and dominant notes of E major are E and B.

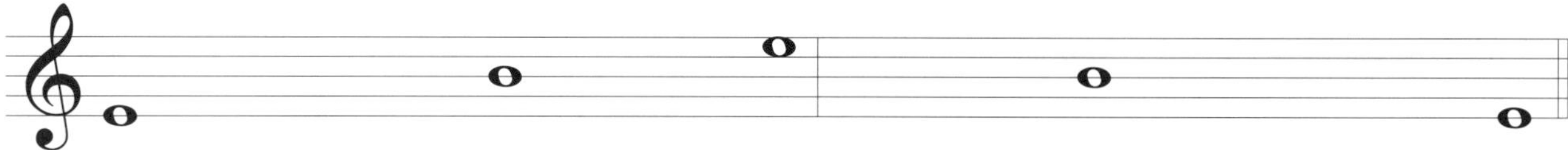

2. Write each of the remaining notes *twice*.

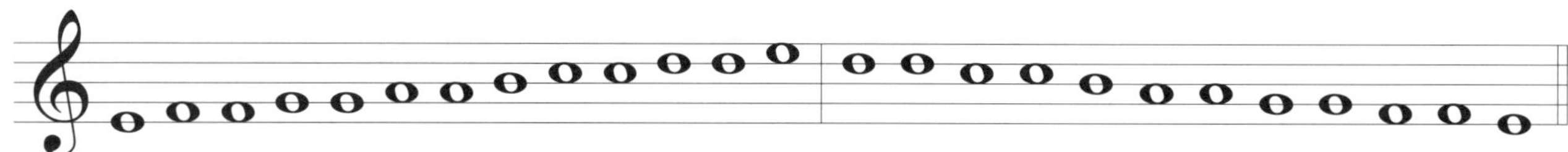

3. Add the necessary accidentals to form a chromatic scale.

To write this type of chromatic scale with a key signature, use the key signature of the major key of the starting note. In the example below, the starting note is E, so we use the key signature of E major. *Note the difference in the pattern of accidentals between this scale and the one above that has no key signature.*

2. Write the following scales, ascending and descending, using a key signature.

Chromatic scale starting on F

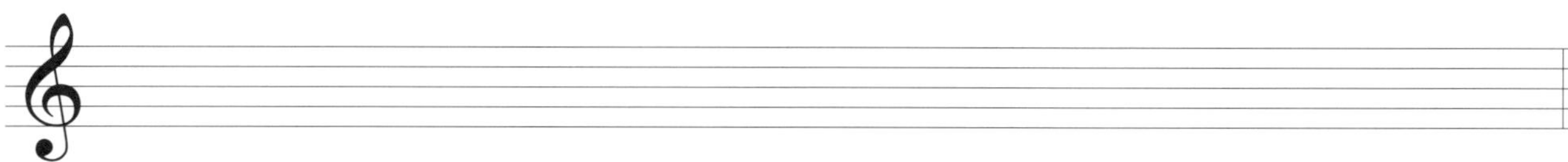

Chromatic scale starting on B

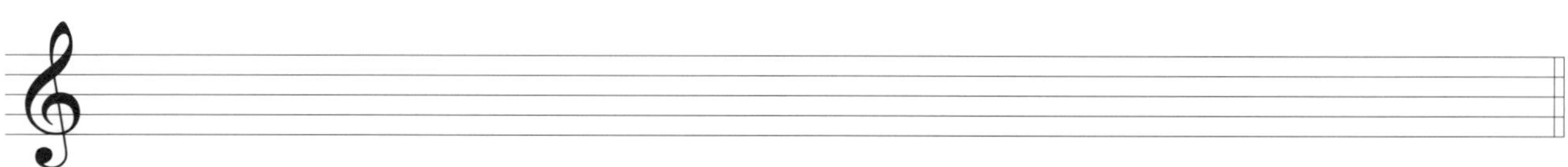

3. Write the following chromatic scales, ascending and descending.

Chromatic scale starting on G

Chromatic scale starting on A♭, using a key signature

Chromatic scale starting on B

Chromatic scale starting on D, using a key signature

Chromatic scale starting on D♭

Chromatic scale starting on G, using a key signature

Chromatic scale starting on F

Chromatic scale starting on C♯, using a key signature

WHOLE TONE SCALES

The **whole tone scale** is made up of whole steps. A whole tone scale can begin on any note, but all whole tone scales are based on one or the other of two forms.

One form starts on C.

The other form starts on C sharp or D flat.

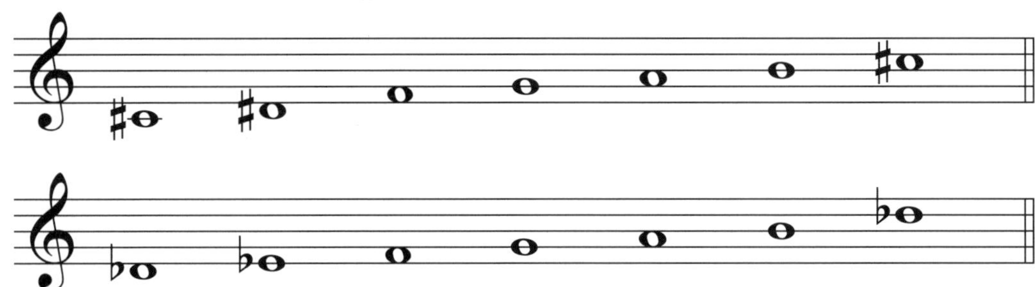

Since the notes of a whole tone scale are spaced evenly, any note can function as a tonic. Music based on a whole tone scale has a feeling of restlessness because of the ambiguity of the tonic. A number of 20th-century composers, including Claude Debussy, used whole tone scales in their music.

The following musical excerpt is an example of a composition based on the whole tone scale. Here, the composer used notes from the whole tone scale beginning on C to create the melody.

Play the whole tone scale that this piece is based on, and then play the excerpt from *Starfish at Night,* listening carefully. What sort of mood is created by the composer's use of whole tones?

Starfish at Night

Source: *Freddie the Frog*
© Copyright 1997 The Frederick Harris Music Co., Limited, Mississauga, Ontario, Canada.

WHOLE TONE SCALES

1. Write the following whole tone scales.

The whole tone scale starting on F

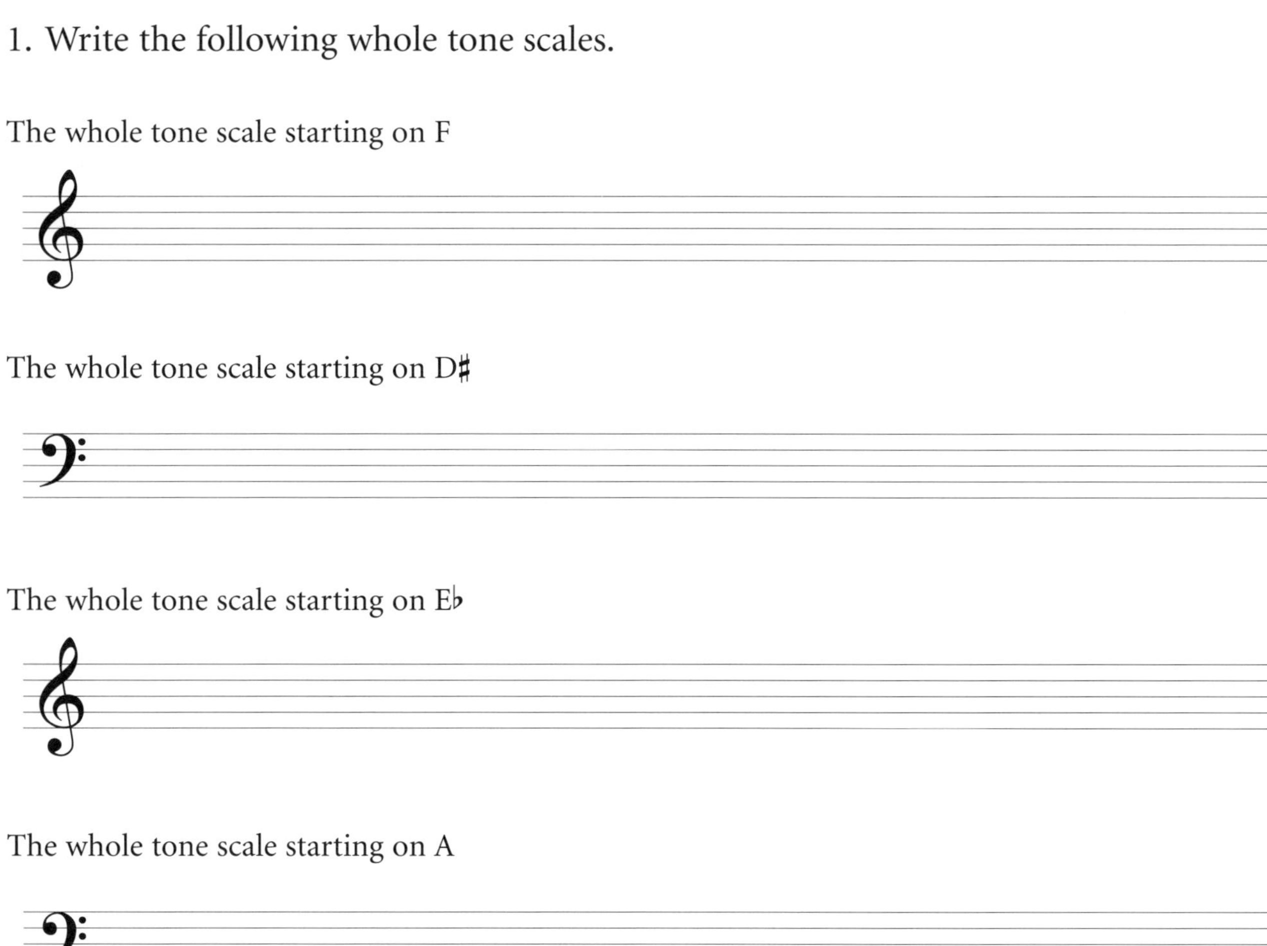

The whole tone scale starting on D♯

The whole tone scale starting on E♭

The whole tone scale starting on A

The Blues Scale

Blues is an African-American music genre characterized by a scale in which certain notes are lowered. A blues tune is usually twelve measures long and consists of three four-measure phrases.

Here is a basic blues scale:

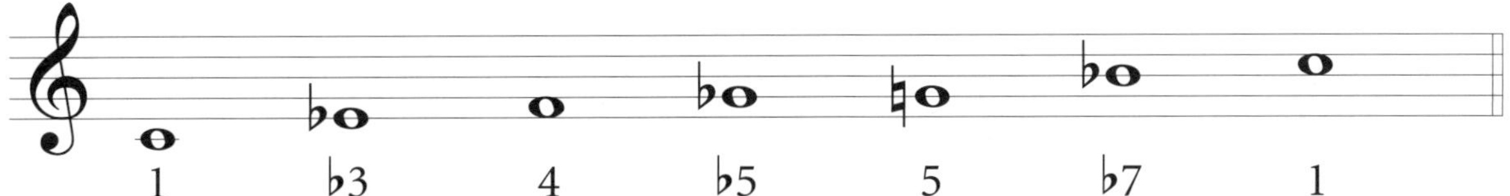

If you compare this scale to a major scale, you will find three differences:

1. The second and sixth degree are missing.
2. The third, fifth, and seventh degrees are lowered by a semitone — these are called "blue" notes.
3. The fifth degree of the scale occurs twice (once unaltered and once lowered).

A blues scale can be formed from a major scale by omitting the second and sixth degrees and lowering the third, fifth and seventh degrees.

1. Write the following blues scales.

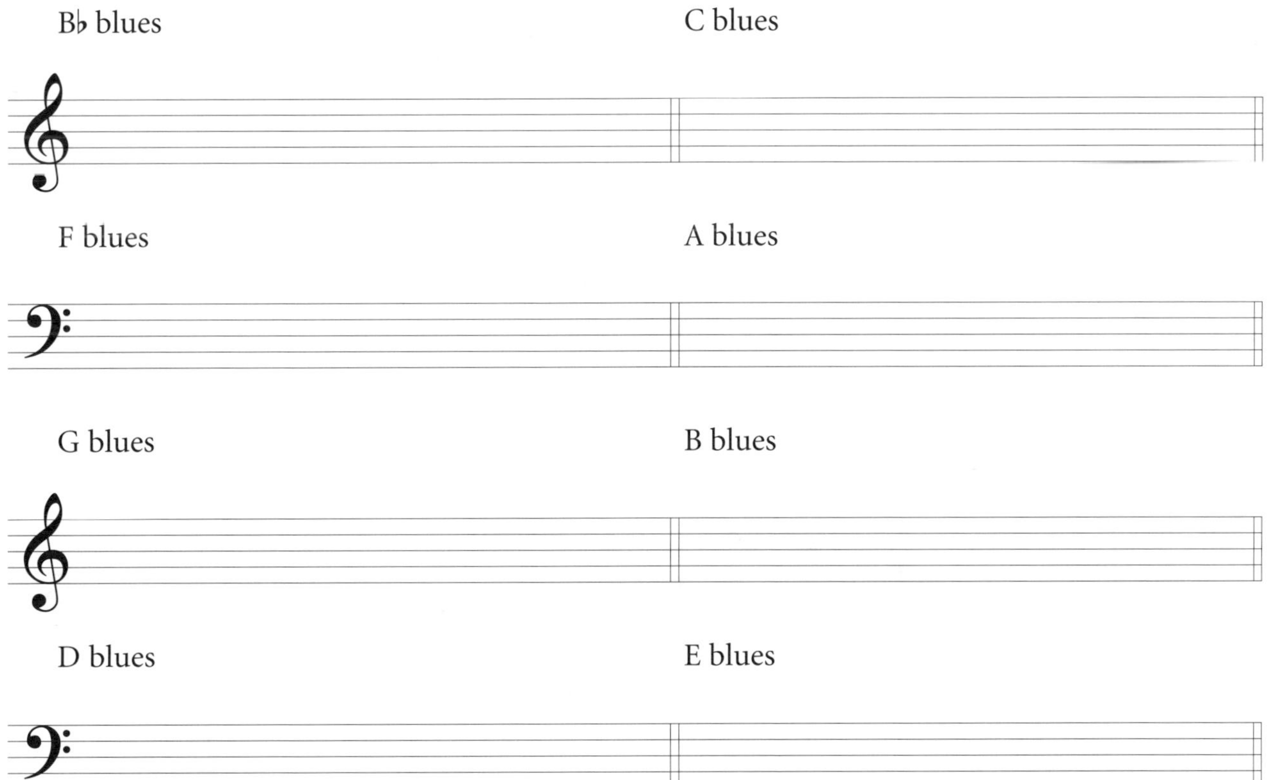

The following piece is an example of the blues in C. The melody of *Gangster Blues* is made up of notes from the C blues scale. Practice the C blues scale and then play *Gangster Blues*. Try playing in swing time. This means playing the eighth notes as if they were a triplet consisting of a quarter and an eighth note.

Using the same left-hand bass part and the C blues scale, improvise your own blues. Use different rhythms and make up your own patterns.

Gangster Blues

Mark Sarnecki

Pentatonic Scales

The **pentatonic scale** consists of five notes, and is one of the oldest scales in existence. It was found in Oriental music as early as 2000 B.C., and is common in folk music. Pentatonic scales were also used by some composers in the 19th and 20th centuries.

A pentatonic scale can be formed by removing the fourth and seventh degrees of a major scale.

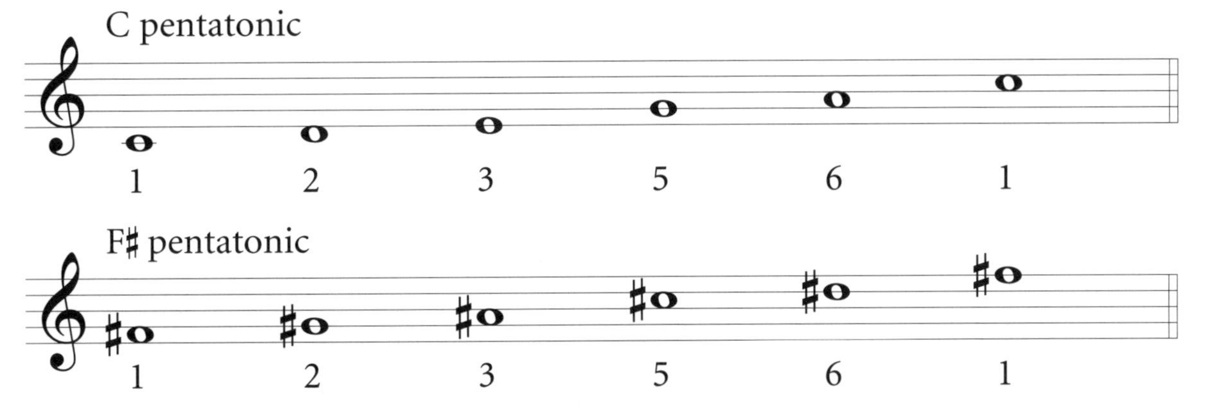

The melody in the following composition is based on the E flat pentatonic scale. Write the E flat pentatonic scale on the staff below. Play the *Bashkir Chastushka* and listen carefully for the pentatonic melody.

Eb pentatonic

Bashkir Chastushka

Source: *Twelve Pieces in Folk Modes*
© Copyright 1995 The Frederick Harris Music Co., Limited, Mississauga, Ontario, Canada.

1. Write the following pentatonic scales.

D pentatonic

A♭ pentatonic

F pentatonic

E pentatonic

B♭ pentatonic

C♯ pentatonic

B pentatonic

G pentatonic

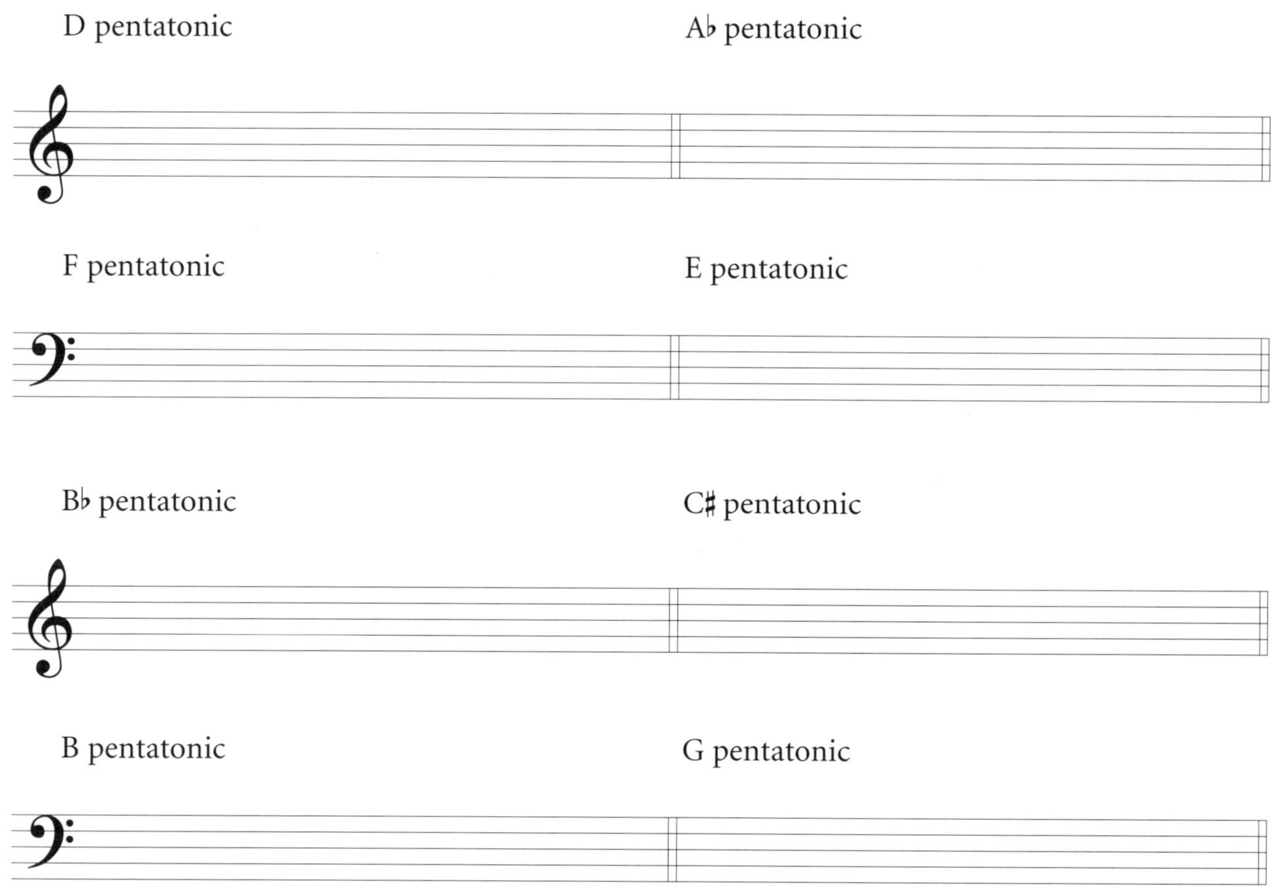

OCTATONIC SCALE

The octatonic scale is an eight-note scale in which tones and semitones alternate. This scale is used prominently in the music of several composers, including Igor Stravinsky. Only three transpositions of the octatonic scale are possible. An octatonic scale starting on any note will have the same pitches as one of the three octatonic scales shown below.

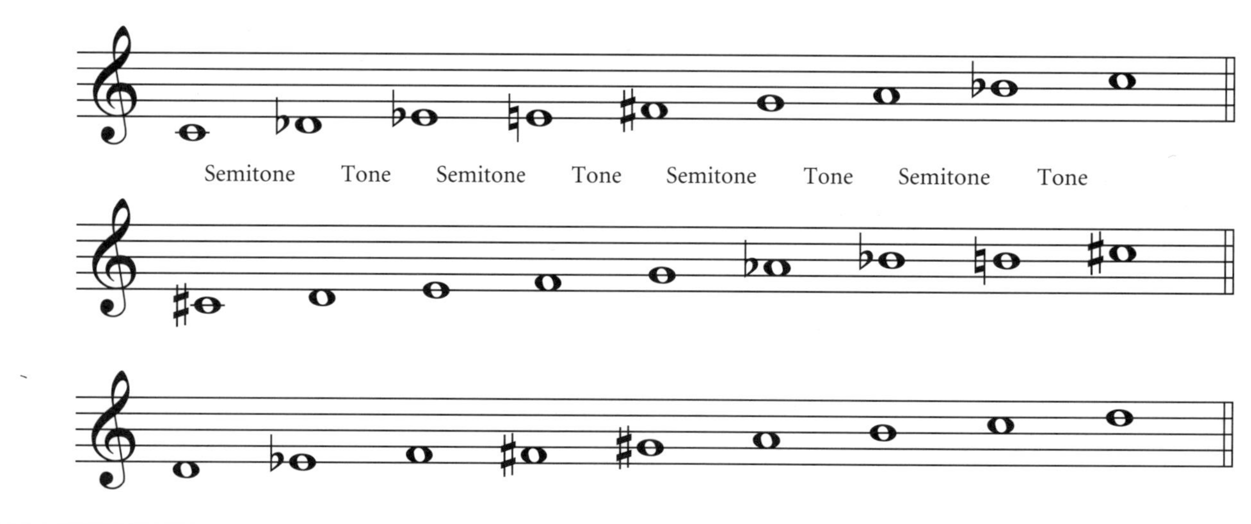

INTERVALS

An interval is the distance between two notes. When the notes of an interval are played one after the other, the interval is called **melodic**.

When the notes of an interval are played at the same time, the interval is called **harmonic.**

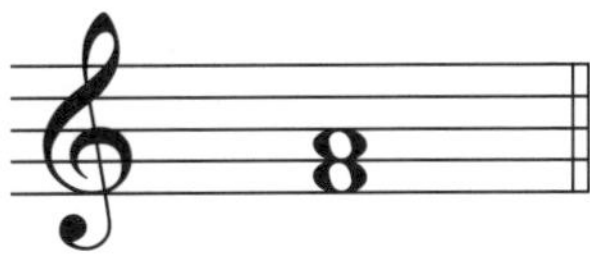

All intervals have a specific number. This number is determined by counting the letter names of the notes in the interval from the lowest to the highest.

There are *five* letter names from C to G.
(C-D-E-F-G)
Therefore, C to G is an interval of a *5th*.

The following intervals are formed between the notes of the major scale.

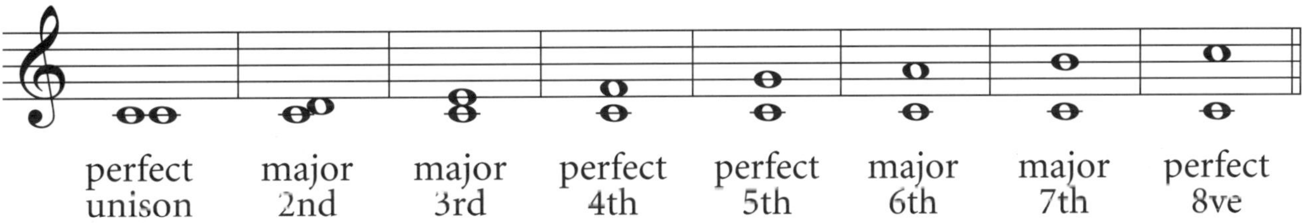

The intervals of a unison, 4th, 5th and octave are classified as **perfect intervals.** The abbreviation for a perfect interval is "per" — for example, per 4.

The intervals of a 2nd, 3rd, 6th and 7th are classified as **major intervals.** The abbreviation for a major interval is "maj" — for example, maj 3.

Think of the bottom note of an interval as the tonic of a major scale. If the upper note of the interval is a member of the scale of the lower note, the interval will be either perfect or major. For example, D to F sharp is a major 3rd because F sharp is the third note of the D major scale. F to B flat is a perfect 4th because B flat is the fourth note of the F major scale.

A **minor interval** is one semitone smaller than a major interval. In other words, the notes of a minor interval are *one semitone closer together* than the notes of a major interval. The abbreviation for a minor interval is "min" — for example, min 3.

Note that only 2nds, 3rds, 6ths, and 7ths can be minor intervals.

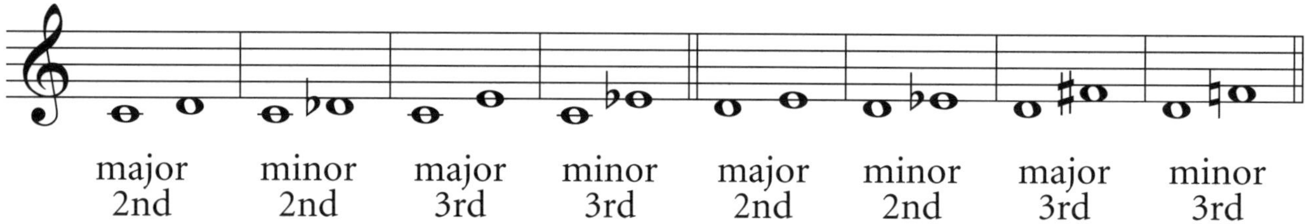

To determine if an interval is major or minor, think of the bottom note as the tonic of a major scale. If the top note is a member of the major scale of the bottom note, the interval is major. If the top note is a semitone lower, the interval is minor.

For example, D to F natural is a 3rd, but F natural is not part of the scale of D major. The interval of D to F natural is one semitone smaller than the major 3rd of D to F sharp. This makes D to F a minor 3rd.

A major interval can be made minor by lowering the top note or raising the bottom note by *one semitone.*

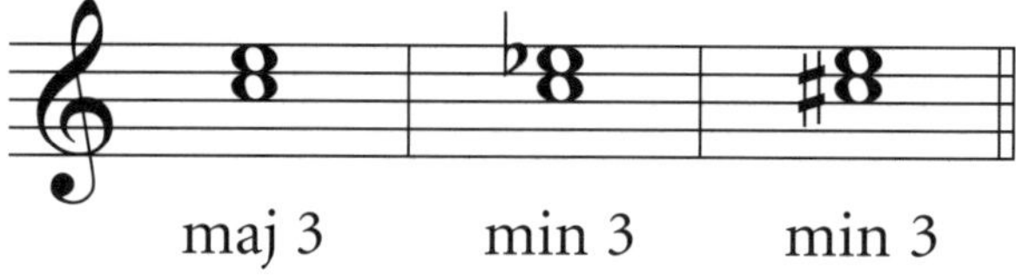

An **augmented interval** is one semitone larger than a perfect or a major interval. In other words, the notes of an augmented interval are one semitone further apart than the notes of a perfect or major interval. The abbreviation for an augmented interval is "aug" — for example, aug 4.

A perfect or major interval can be made augmented by raising the top note or lowering the bottom note by one semitone.

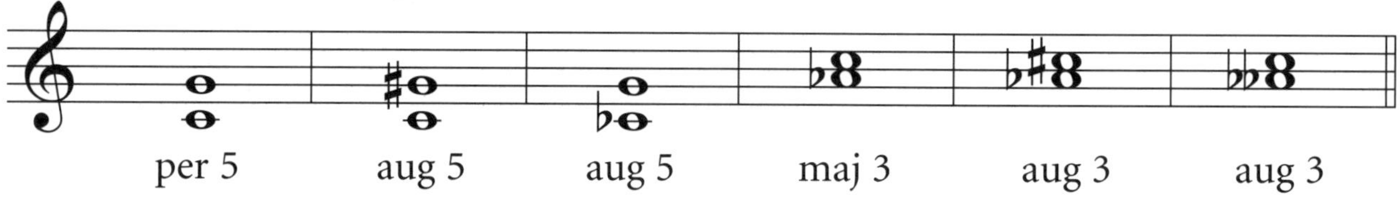

A **diminished interval** is one semitone smaller than either a *perfect interval* or a *minor interval*. In other words, the notes of a diminished interval are one semitone closer together than the notes of either a perfect or minor interval. The abbreviation for a diminished interval is "dim" — for example, dim 5.

A *perfect* interval can be made diminished by lowering the top note or raising the bottom note by *one semitone*.

A *minor* interval can be made diminished by lowering the top note or raising the bottom note by *one semitone*.

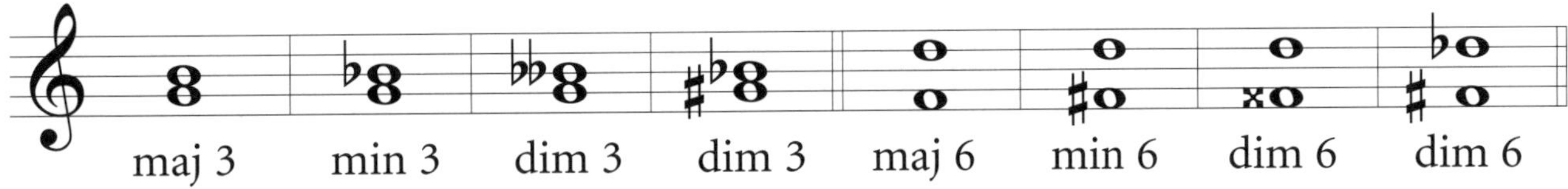

Note that a diminished interval is *one semitone smaller than a perfect interval*, but *two semitones smaller than a major interval*.

Here is a summary of the relationship between the various types of intervals. The starting point is the note in the major scale.

MINUS ⬅ two semitones	MINUS ⬅ one semitone	Note in the MAJOR SCALE	➡ PLUS one semitone
	Diminished unison, 4th, 5th, 8ve	**Perfect** unison, 4th, 5th, 8ve	**Augmented** unison, 4th, 5th, 8ve
Diminished 2nd, 3rd, 6th, 7th	**Minor** 2nd, 3rd, 6th, 7th	**Major** 2nd, 3rd, 6th, 7th	**Augmented** 2nd, 3rd, 6th, 7th

1. Name the following intervals, then rewrite each as an augmented interval by changing the upper note.

2. Name the following intervals, then rewrite each as an augmented interval by changing the bottom note.

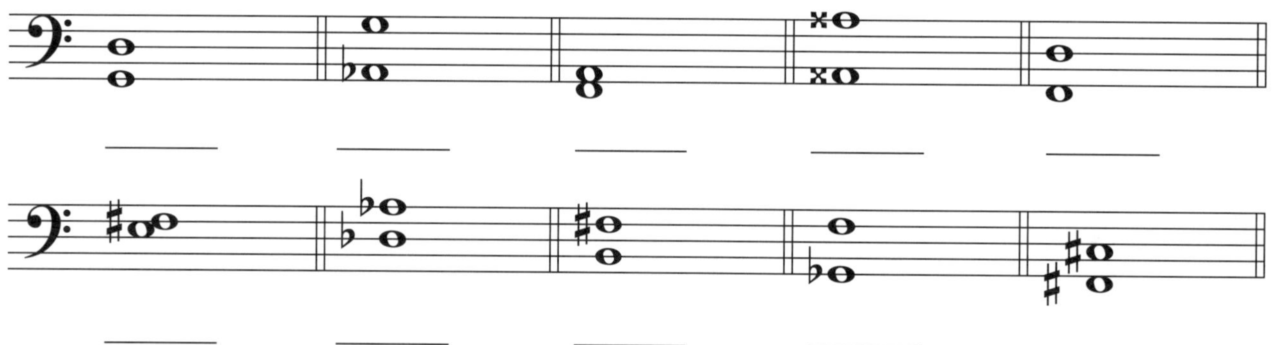

3. Name the following intervals, then rewrite each as a diminished interval by changing the top note.

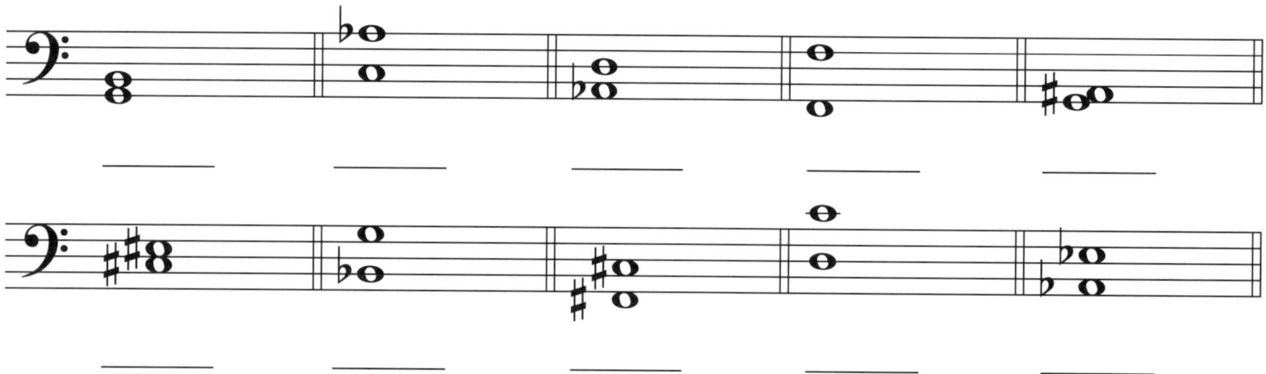

4. Name the following intervals, then rewrite each as a diminished interval by changing the bottom note.

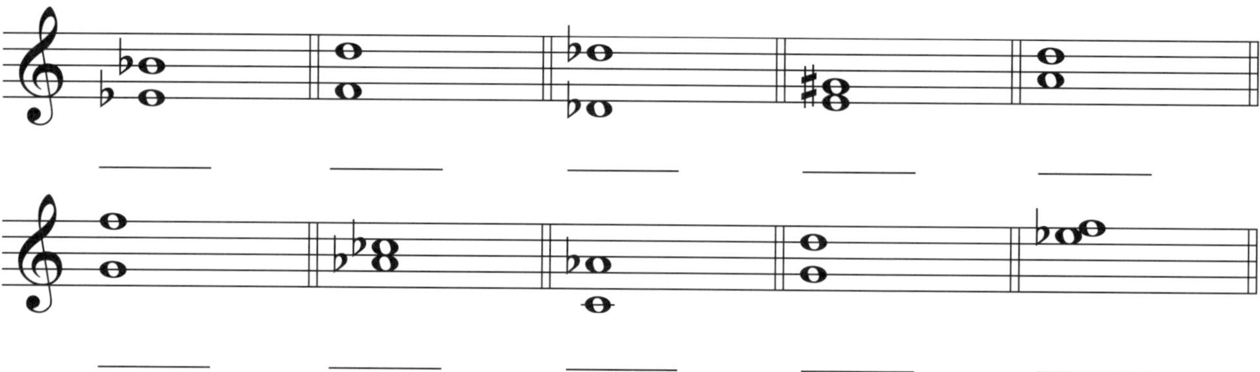

5. Write the following intervals above the given notes.

maj 3   aug 4   min 6   dim 5   per 8   dim 7   aug 2

maj 3   aug 4   min 6   dim 5   per 8   dim 7   aug 2

maj 3   aug 4   min 6   dim 5   per 8   dim 7   aug 2

maj 3   aug 4   min 6   dim 5   per 8   dim 7   aug 2

Sometimes the lowest note of an interval is not the tonic of a major key. For instance, in the example below, we know that D sharp to A sharp is a 5th, but there is no such key as D sharp major.

In order to name the interval, we must follow three steps:

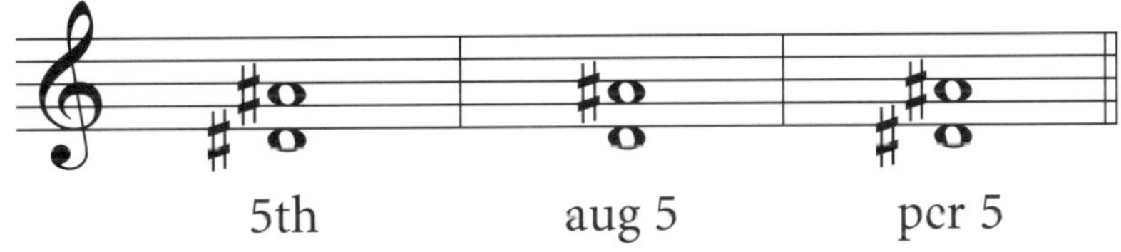

1. Lower the bottom note to the note that is the tonic of an existing key. *Note that this note has the same letter name, so the number of the interval remains the same.* In the example above, we lowered D sharp one semitone to D.

2. Name the new interval. The interval of D to A sharp is an augmented 5th.

3. Move the lower note back up to its original pitch. By raising the lower note, we have made the interval one semitone smaller. A perfect 5th is one semitone smaller than an augmented 5th, so the interval of D sharp to A sharp must be a perfect 5th.

1. Name the following intervals.

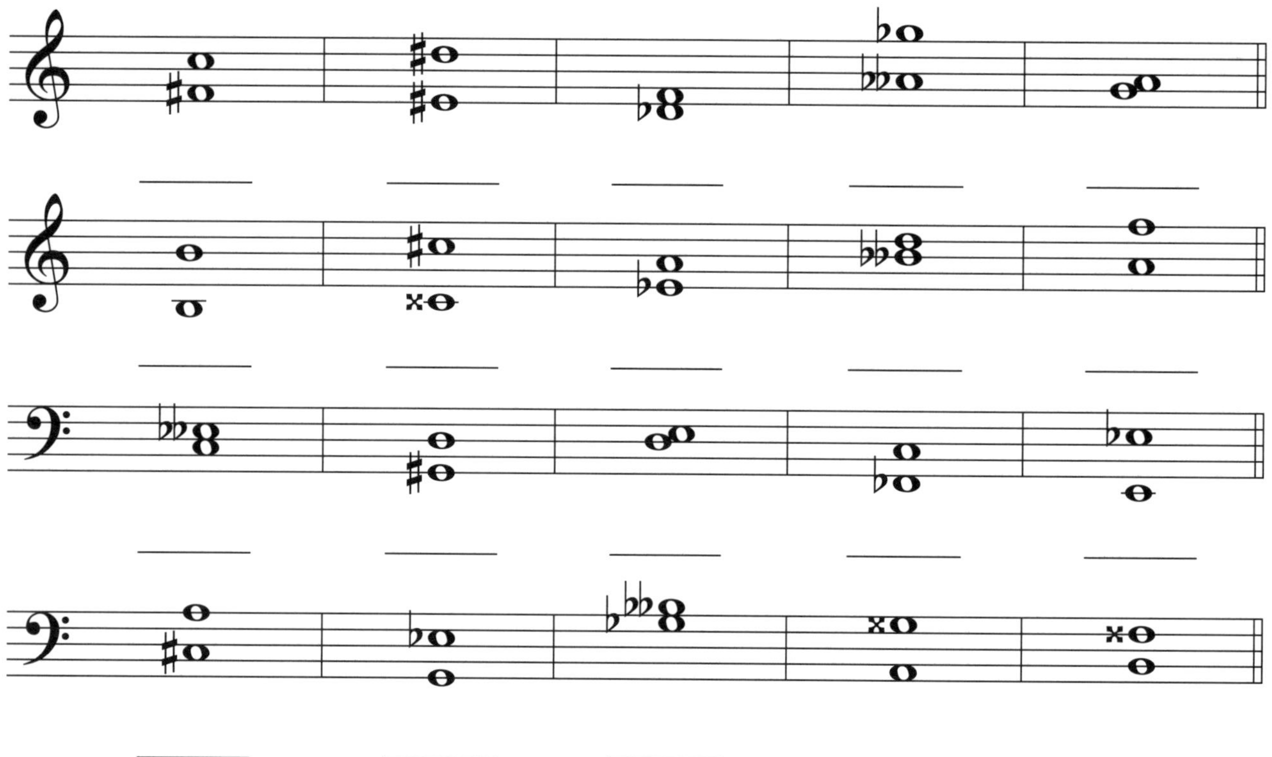

Inversion

When an interval is turned upside down, it is **inverted.** For example, when the interval of G to B is inverted, it becomes B to G.

There are two ways to invert an interval:
1. Write the lower note above the upper note.
2. Write the upper note below the lower note.

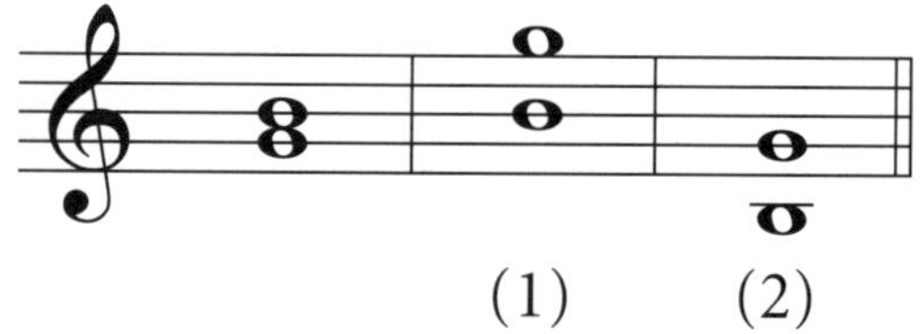

When an interval is inverted:

major	becomes	**minor**
minor	becomes	**major**
augmented	becomes	**diminished**
diminished	becomes	**augmented**
perfect	remains	**perfect**

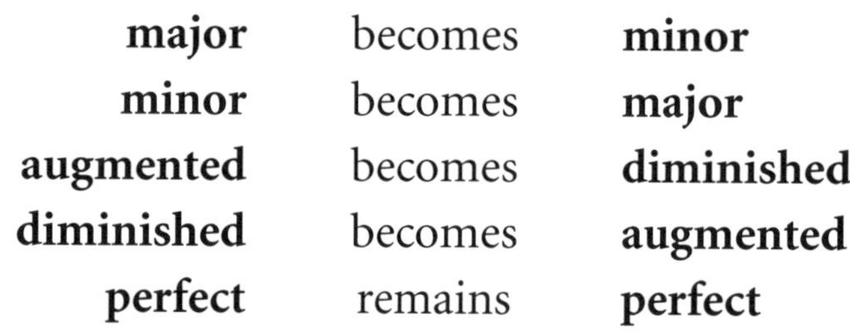

Note that the number of an interval *plus* the number of its inversion always equals nine.

2. Name the following intervals. Invert them and name the inversions.

3. Write the following intervals above the given notes. Invert each interval and name the inversion.

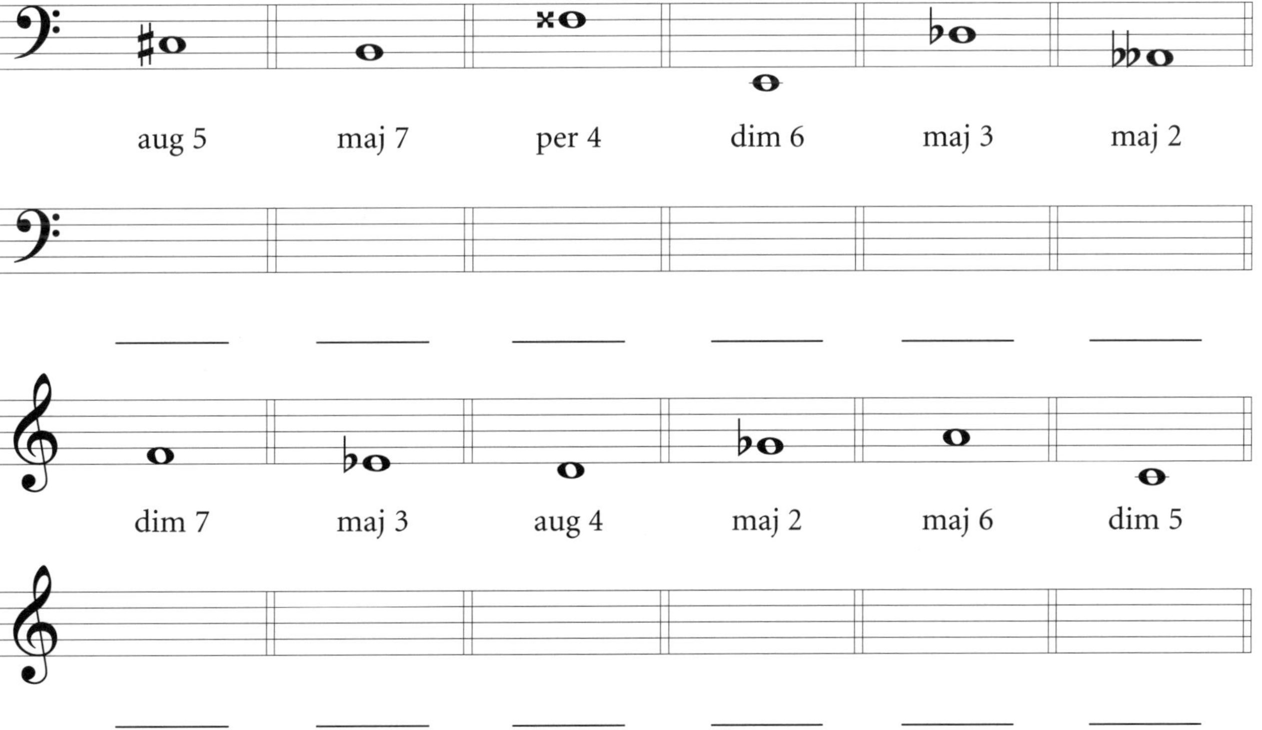

INTERVALS

4. Write the following intervals above the given notes.

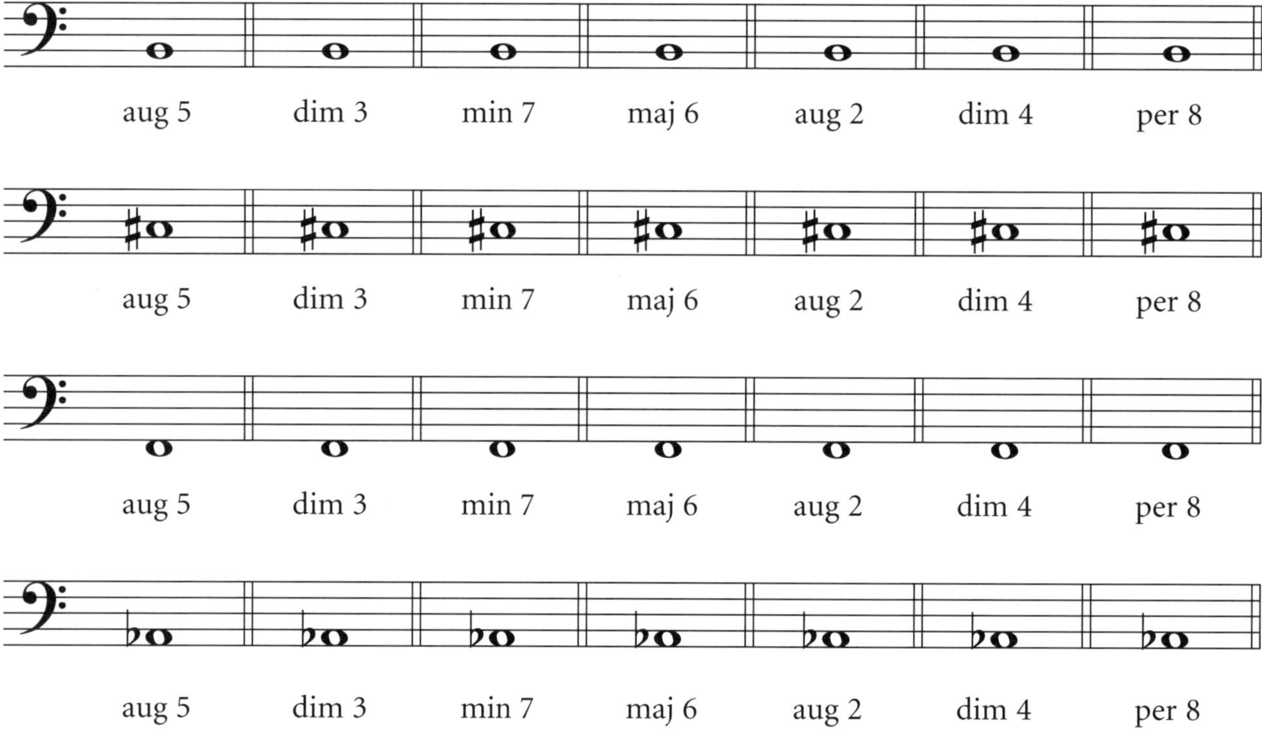

5. Learn the following Italian terms and their translations or definitions.

accelerando	becoming quicker
a tempo	return to the previous tempo
alla	in the manner of
assai	much, very much (for example, *allegro assai*: very fast)
ben	well
col, colla	with
coll'ottava	with an added octave
con moto	with movement

REVIEW 1

1. Fill in the blanks.

Major key	Key signature	Relative minor key
C♯ major	__________________	__________
G♭ major	__________________	__________
F♯ major	__________________	__________
B major	__________________	__________
D♭ major	__________________	__________
C♭ major	__________________	__________

2. Write the following key signatures.

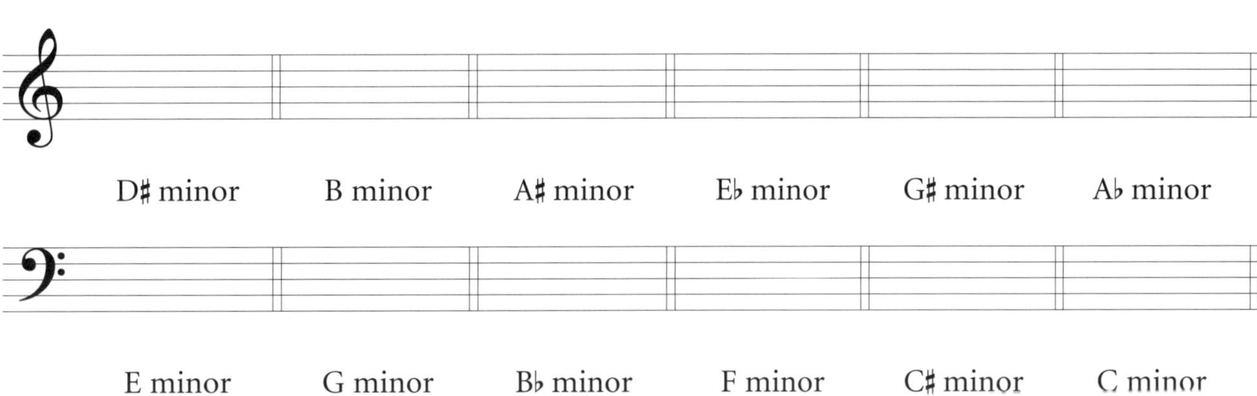

3. Write the following notes using key signatures.

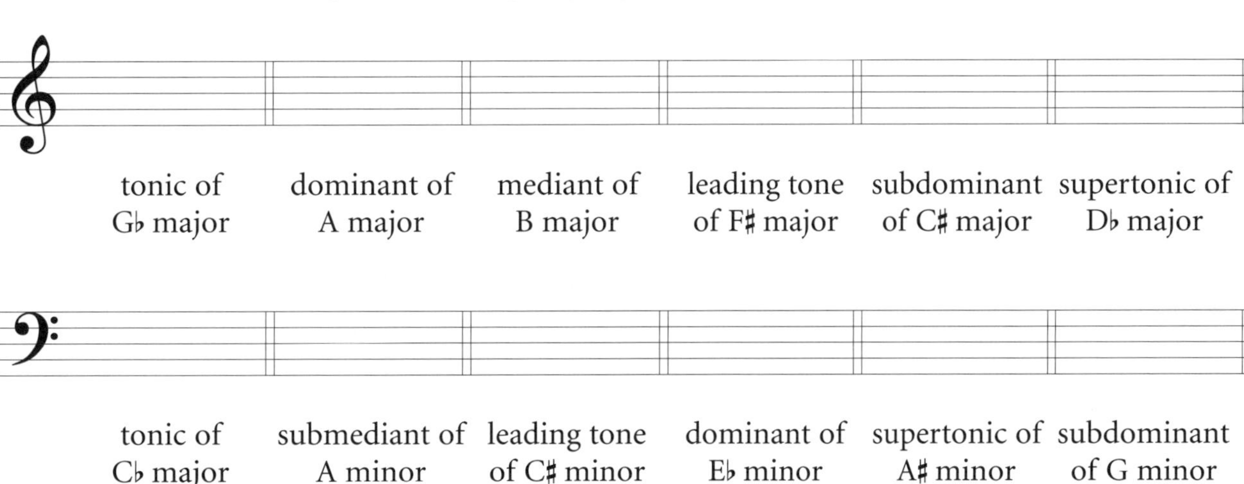

4. Write the following scales in half notes, ascending and descending, using key signatures.

30

The major scale with C♯ as the supertonic

The major scale with a key signature of six flats

The harmonic minor scale with A♯ as the dominant

The melodic minor scale with a key signature of five flats

The major scale with B♭ as the leading tone

The harmonic minor scale with A♭ as the tonic

The melodic minor scale with a key signature of three sharps

The major scale with B♭ as the subdominant

The harmonic minor scale with E♭ as the mediant

The melodic minor scale with a key signature of two sharps

5. Name the following intervals. Invert them and name the inversions.

18

_____   _____   _____   _____   _____   _____

_____   _____   _____   _____   _____   _____

6. Match the following terms with their definitions.

16

tranquillo	_____	(a) in the manner of
animato	_____	(b) light, nimble, quick
ben	_____	(c) with movement
leggiero	_____	(d) return to the previous tempo
espressivo	_____	(e) brilliant
con brio	_____	(f) lively, animated
con moto	_____	(g) with
con espressione	_____	(h) quiet, tranquil
col, colla	_____	(i) well
alla	_____	(j) becoming quicker
brillante	_____	(k) with an added octave
accelerando	_____	(l) with expression
coll' ottava	_____	(m) much, very much
a tempo	_____	(n) with vigour, spirit
con	_____	(o) expressive, with expression
assai	_____	(p) with

TIME

In **compound time**, the basic beat is a dotted note. Time signatures in compound time have 6 (compound duple), 9 (compound triple), or 12 (compound quadruple) as the upper number.

In **compound duple time**, there are two beats in each measure. A beat is a group of three pulses and is represented by a dotted note. The upper number of the time signature is always 6, which indicates that each measure contains six pulses (two beats of three pulses). The lower number, which indicates the note that receives one pulse, can be 4, 8, or 16.

6 4 six pulses or two beats in each measure
the quarter note receives one pulse

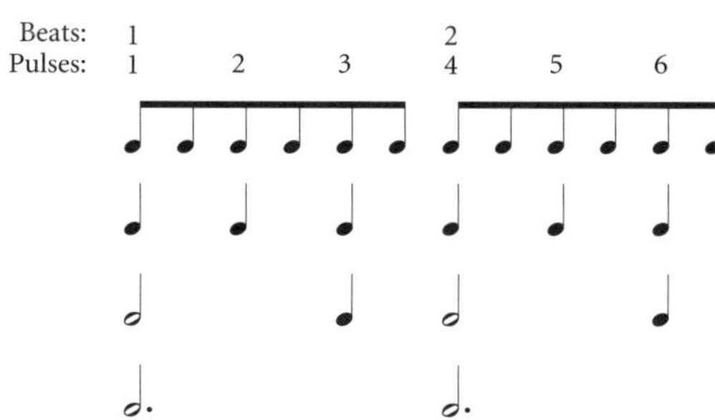

6 8 six pulses or two beats in each measure
the eighth note receives one pulse

6 16 six pulses or two beats in each measure
the sixteenth note receives one pulse

In **compound triple time**, there are three beats in each measure. The upper number of the time signature is always 9, which indicates that each measure contains nine pulses (three beats of three pulses). The lower number, which indicates the note that receives one pulse, can be 4, 8, or 16.

9/4 nine pulses (three beats) in each measure
the quarter note receives one pulse

9/8 nine pulses (three beats) in each measure
the eighth note receives one pulse

9/16 nine pulses (three beats) in each measure
the sixteenth note receives one pulse

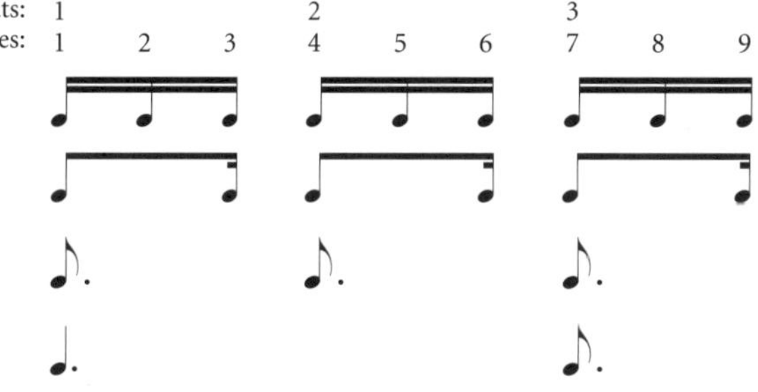

In **compound quadruple time**, there are four beats in each measure. The upper number of the time signature is always 12, which indicates that each measure contains twelve pulses (four beats of three pulses). The lower number, which indicates the note that receives one pulse, can be 4, 8, or 16.

12/4 — twelve pulses (four beats) in each measure; the quarter note receives one pulse

12/8 — twelve pulses (four beats) in each measure; the eighth note receives one pulse

12/16 — twelve pulses (four beats) in each measure; the sixteenth note receives one pulse

1. Add time signatures to the following one-measure rhythms. Circle each beat
    (group of three pulses).

2. Add bar lines to the following melodies.

Rests

In compound time, as in simple time, a whole rest is used to indicate an entire measure of silence in any time signature.

Remember that notes are grouped in three-pulse patterns in compound time. Rests must also follow this three-pulse pattern.

When adding rests to complete the *first two pulses* of a three-pulse group in compound time, *use one rest.*

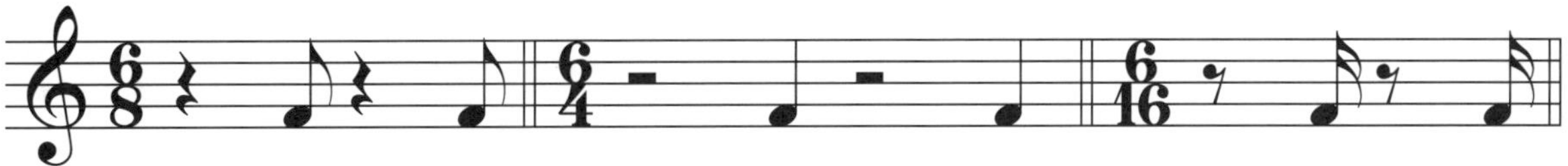

When adding rests to complete the *last two pulses* of a three-pulse group in compound time, *use two rests.*

In **compound triple time,** you may *join beats one and two,* but *do not join beats two and three.*

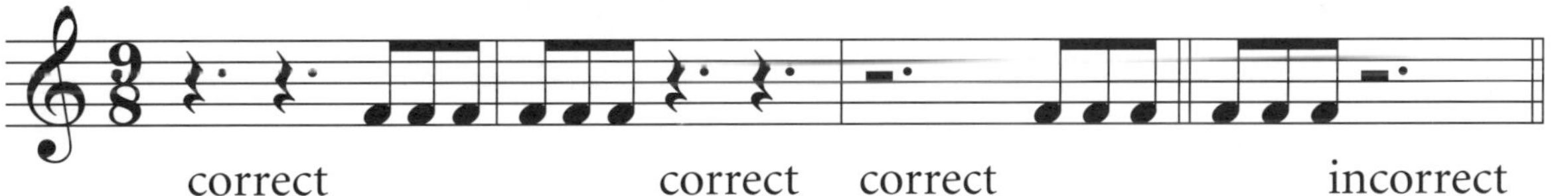

In **compound quadruple time,** you may *complete the first or last half of the bar with one dotted rest. Do not join beats two and three into one rest.*

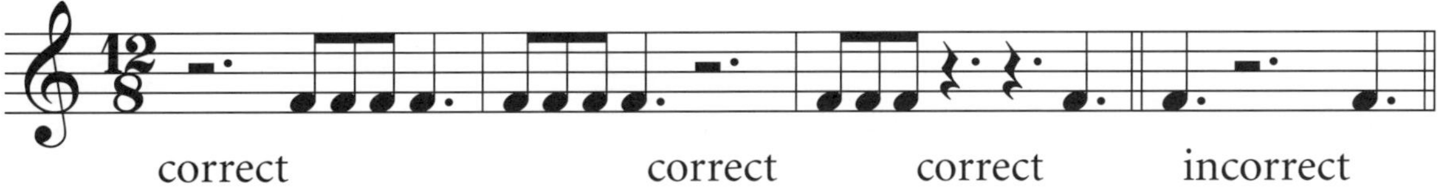

1. Add rests under the brackets according to the time signatures.

Simple Duple Time
Compound Duple Time
Simple Triple Time
Compound Triple Time
Simple Quadruple Time
Compound Quadruple Time

The **thirty-second** and **sixty-fourth** notes and rests are written as follows:

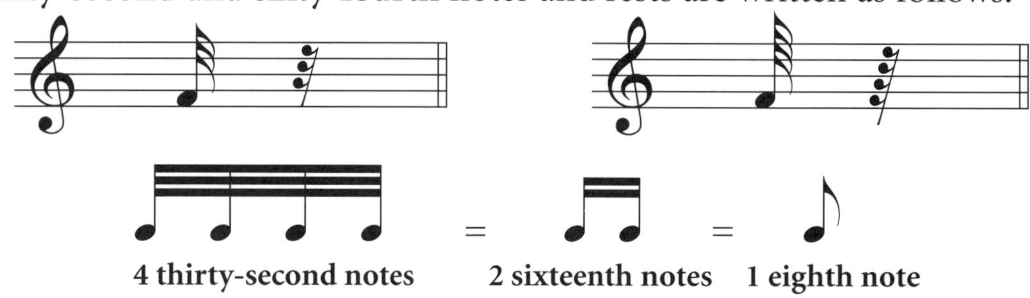

Triplets

A **triplet** is a group of three notes that are played in the time of two notes of the same value. They are most frequently found in simple time.

Triplets are always indicated by a "*3*". Here are some examples of different ways triplets can be written.

Here are some examples of the different ways triplets can be used:

(a)  The *three* eighth notes played in the time of *two* eighth notes equal one beat.

(b)  *Three* sixteenth notes played in the time of *two* sixteenth notes equal one half beat.

(c) 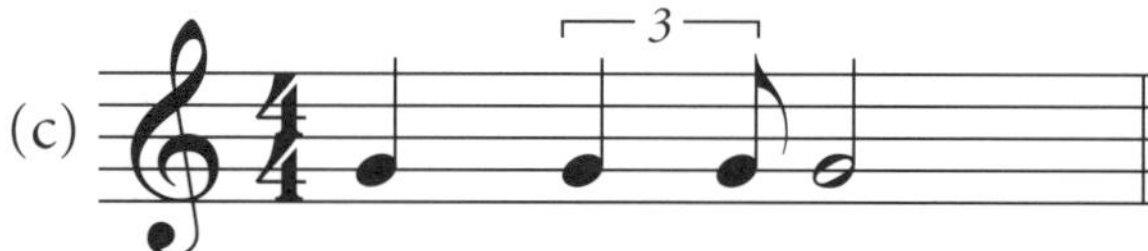 This triplet has only two notes. Together, the quarter and the eighth notes are equal to *three* eighth notes, but they are played in the time of *two* eighth notes.

(d)  This triplet has a dotted rhythm. Once again, the three-note rhythm is equal to *three* eighth notes that are played in the time of *two* eighth notes.

Double Dots

A second dot after a note is worth half the value of the first dot.

1. Add time signatures to the following one-measure rhythms. The rhythms may be in simple or compound time.

Irregular Groups

A **duplet** is a group of *two* notes that are played in the time of *three* notes of the same value. Duplets are found in *compound time*.

A **quadruplet** is a group of *four* notes that are played in the time of *three* notes of the same value. Quadruplets are found in *compound time*.

A **quintuplet** is a group of *five* notes that are played in the time of *three, four, or six* notes of the same value, depending on the time signature.

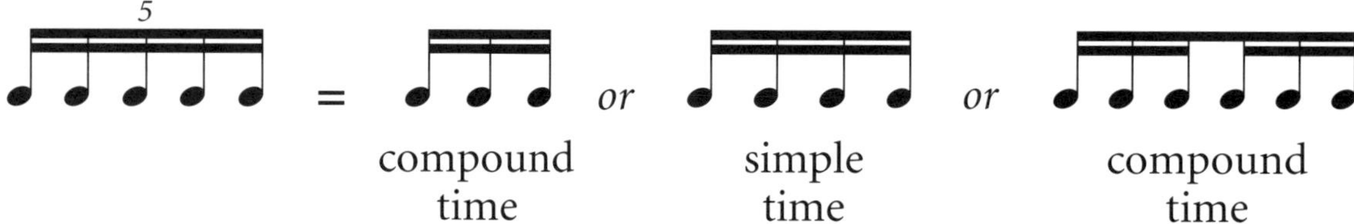

A **sextuplet** is a group of *six* notes that are played in the time of *four* notes of the same value.

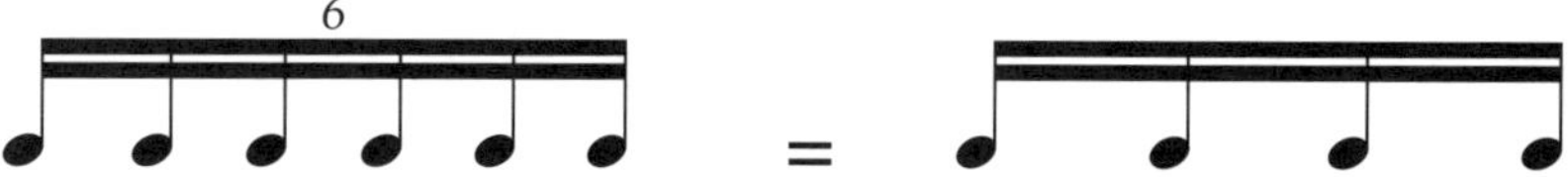

A **septuplet** is a group of *seven* notes that are played in the time of *three* or *four* notes of the same value, depending on the time signature.

To determine the value of an irregular group of notes, examine the remaining beats (and partial beats) in the measure. The irregular group will fill the remaining beats (or partial beats) required to complete the measure.

1. Add bar lines to the following melodies according to the time signatures.

2. Add rests under the brackets according to the time signatures.

Syncopation

Syncopation occurs when the pattern of strong and weak beats in a measure is altered, and the accent is shifted from the strong beat to the weak beat.

3. Write three-measure rhythms for the following time signatures. (Use a different rhythm for each measure.)

4. Add time signatures to the following one-measure rhythms.

5. Add rests under the brackets according to the time signatures.

6. Add stems to the following note heads, and group them to create one-measure rhythms according to the time signatures.

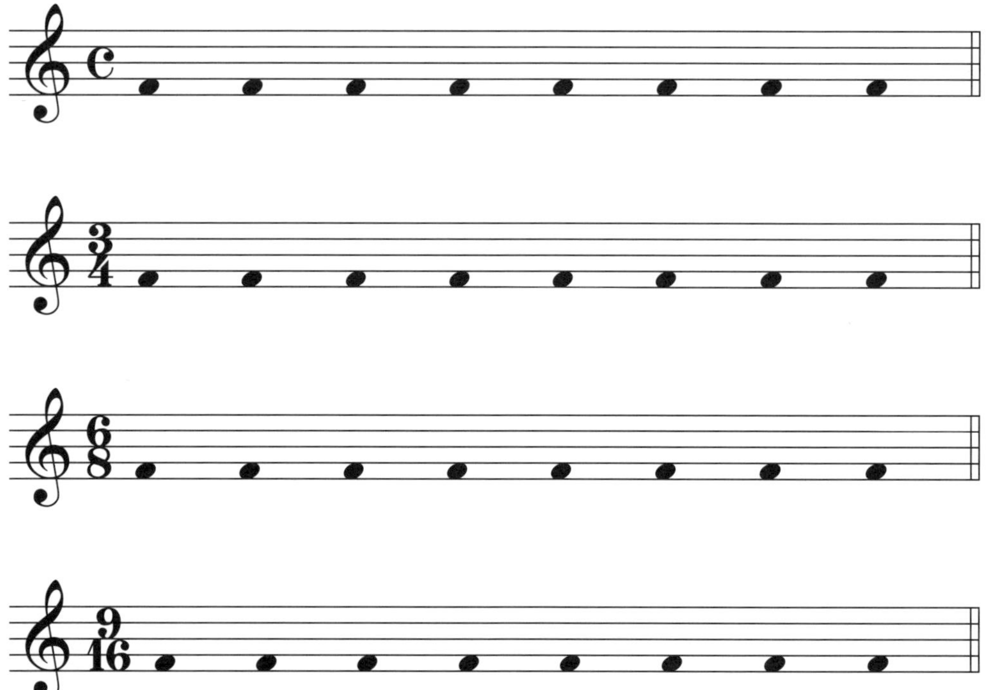

7. Learn the following Italian terms and their definitions.

non	not
non troppo	not too much
ottava, 8va	the interval of an octave
più	more
più mosso	more movement (quicker)
poco	little
poco a poco	little by little
quasi	almost, as if
sempre	always, continuously

*R*EVIEW *2*

1. The following scales start on degrees other than the tonic. For each scale:

   (a) name the key and the type of scale (major, harmonic or melodic minor)
   (b) name the degree of the scale on which the scale begins

(a) _________________________________ (b) _________________________________

(a) _________________________________ (b) _________________________________

(a) _________________________________ (b) _________________________________

(a) _________________________________ (b) _________________________________

(a) _________________________________ (b) _________________________________

2. Define the following Italian terms.

accelerando ____

con moto ____

assai ____

non troppo ____

sempre ____

3. Write the following intervals using F sharp as the lowest note for each.

10

    major 6th   minor 3rd   perfect 5th   augmented 2nd   diminished 4th

4. Invert the above intervals and name the inversions.

10

__________   __________   __________   __________   __________

5. Write the following notes using key signatures.

20

    supertonic of   dominant of   leading tone of   mediant of   subdominant of
    F♯ major   A major   D minor   E♭ minor   D♭ major

    submediant of   tonic of   dominant of   supertonic of   leading tone of
    B minor   B major   C♯ minor   of F minor   E minor

6. Name the relative major of the following minor keys.

10

D minor____   C minor_______________________________________

C♯ minor ____   B minor_______________________________________

G minor____   F♯ minor __________________________________

E♭ minor ____   F minor ___________________________________

A♭ minor ____   B♭ minor _________________________________

7. Complete the following measures by adding rests under the brackets.

10

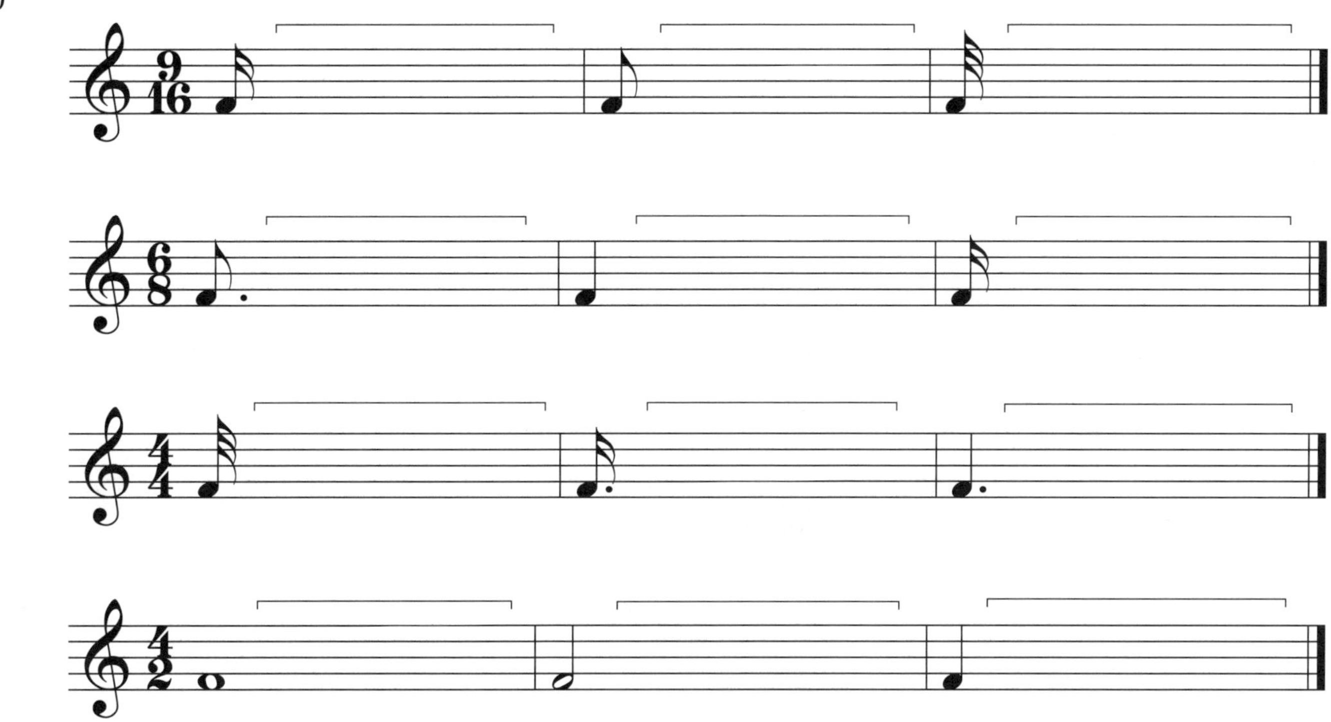

8. Add time signatures to the following rhythms.

10

CHORDS

A **triad** is a three-note chord. The three notes of a triad are called the **root,** the **third** and the **fifth.**

A **major triad** consists of the intervals of a **major 3rd** and a **perfect 5th** above the root. In the F major triad below, F to A is a major 3rd and F to C is a perfect 5th.

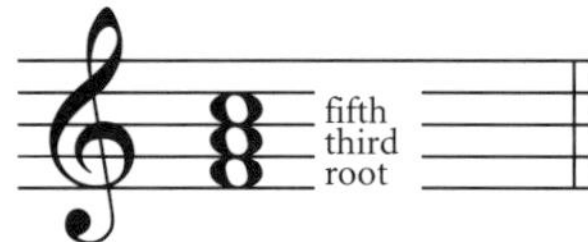

A **minor triad** consists of the intervals of a **minor 3rd** and a **perfect 5th** above the root. In the F minor triad below, F to A flat is a minor 3rd and F to C is a perfect 5th.

A triad can be built on any degree of a major or minor scale.

Triads can occur in three different positions:

1.   If the *root* of the chord is the lowest note, the triad is in *root position.*

2.   If the *third* of the chord is the lowest note, the triad is in *first inversion.*

3.   If the *fifth* of the chord is the lowest note, the triad is in *second inversion.*

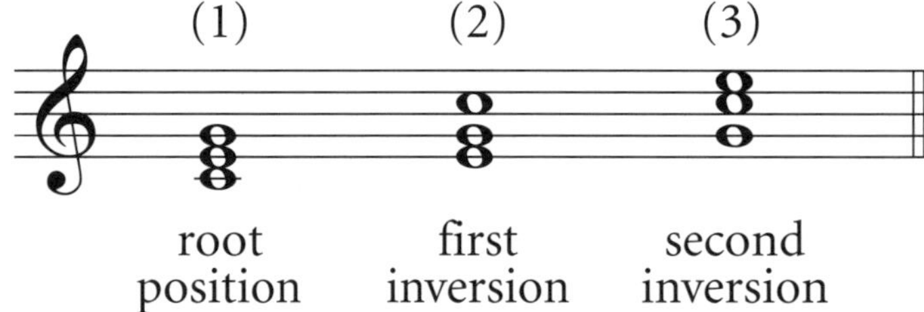

The inversions of the triad are created by raising the bottom note one octave. In the example above, moving C up one octave from root position creates the first inversion. Moving E up one octave from the first inversion creates the second inversion.

1. Identify the following triads as major (maj) or minor (min).

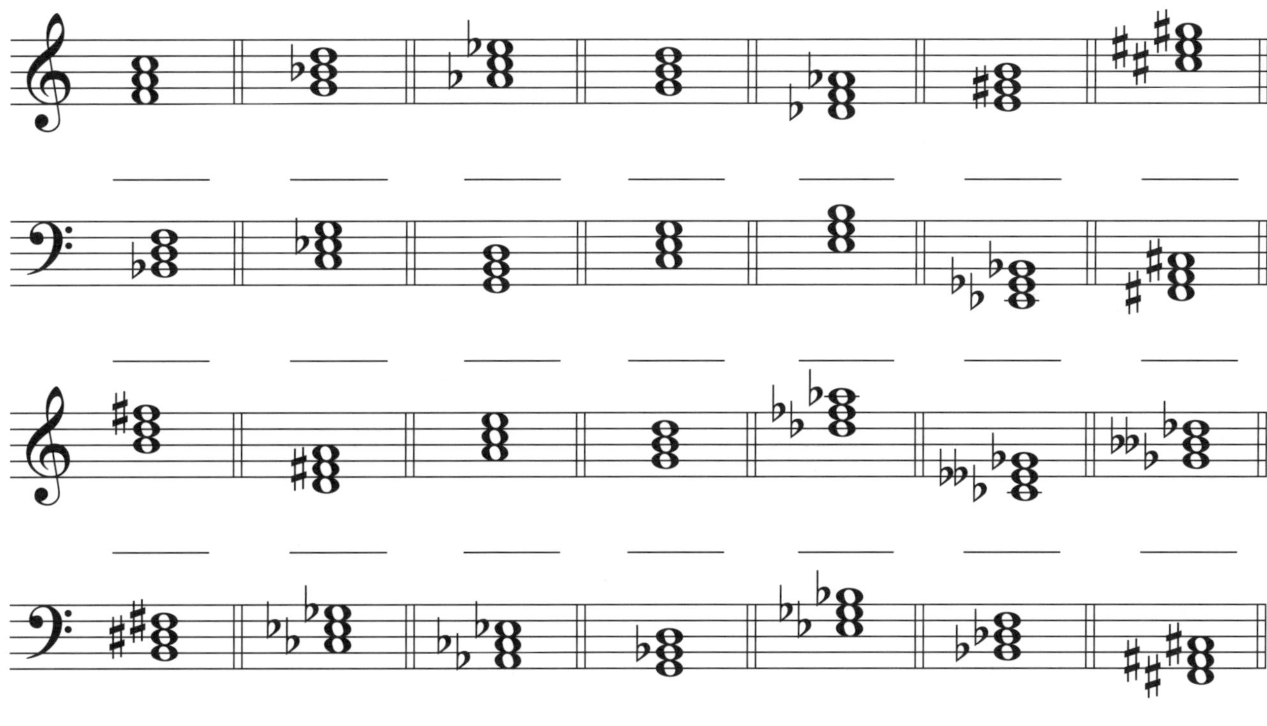

You may be asked to identify a given triad. Here are three steps to determine the root, the type, and the position of a triad.

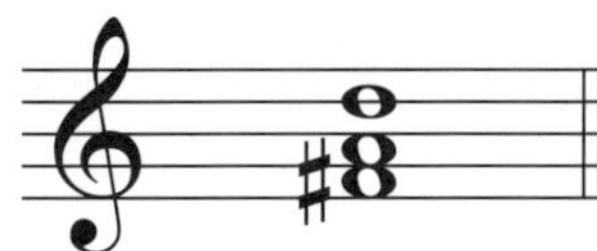

1. Put the triad in root position. In other words, rearrange the notes so that they are a 3rd apart. In root position, the bottom note of the triad is the root.

    In the example below, the bottom note — D — is the root.

2. Identify the intervals between the root and the third, and between the root and the fifth. This will tell you the type of triad (major or minor).

    In the example below, the triad consists of a major 3rd and a perfect 5th. Therefore, it is a major triad.

3. Look at the lowest note of the given triad. If this note is the root, the triad is in root position. If it is the 3rd, the triad is in first inversion. If it is the 5th, the triad is in second inversion.

    In the given triad, the lowest note — F sharp — is the third of the triad. Therefore, this triad is in first inversion.

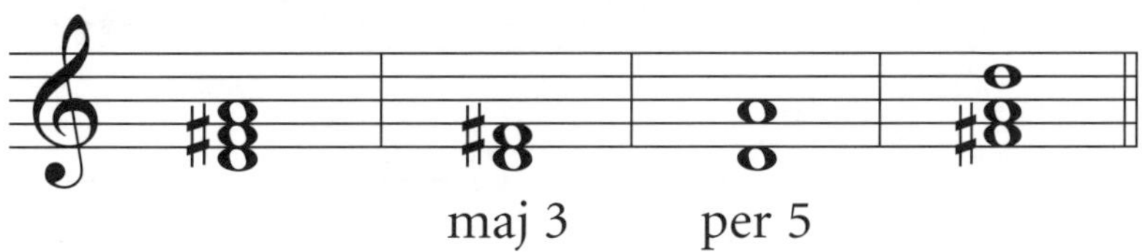

2. Write major triads in root position above the given notes. In the measures that follow, write the triads in first and second inversion.

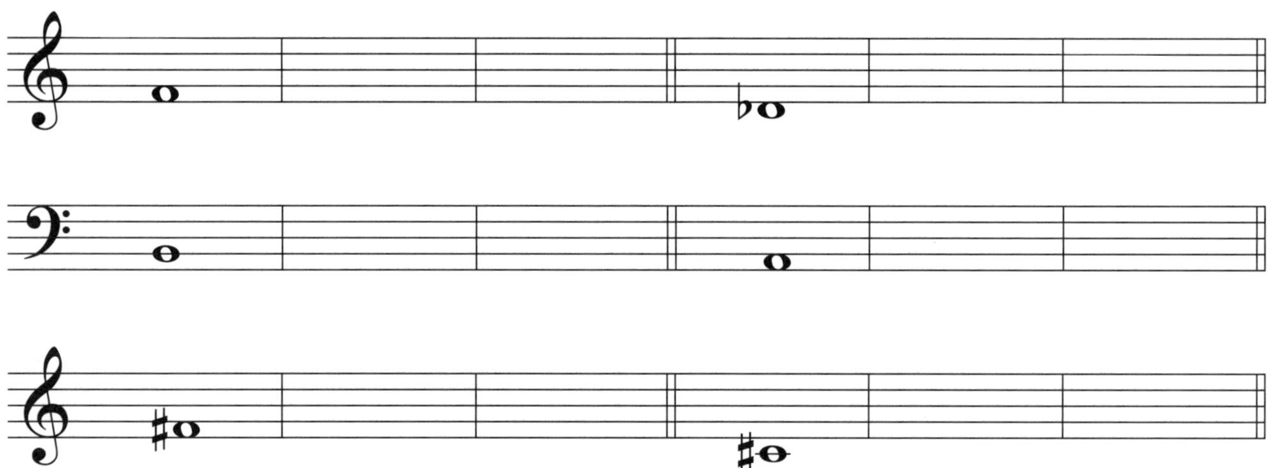

3. Write minor triads in root position above the given notes. In the measures that follow, write the triads in first and second inversion.

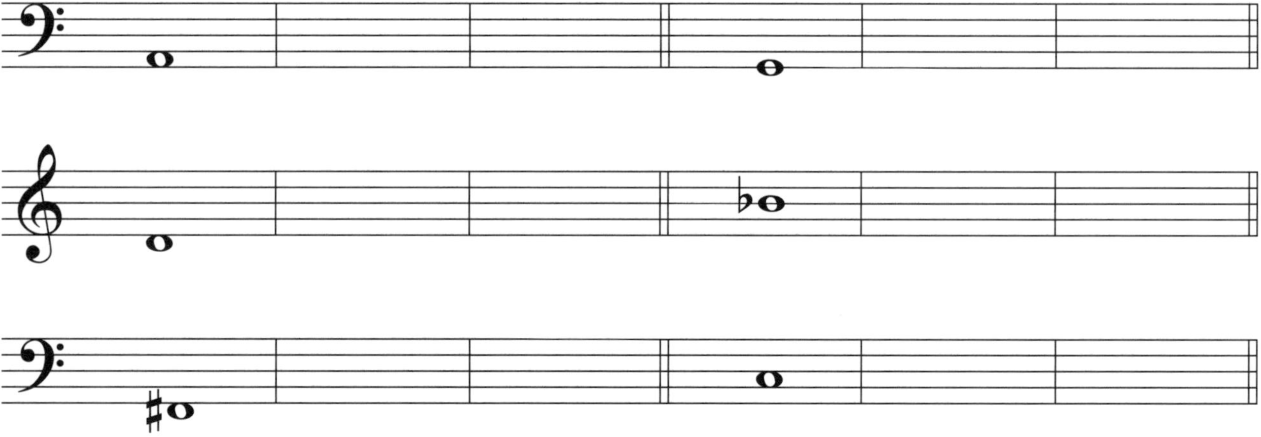

4. Name the roots of the following triads.

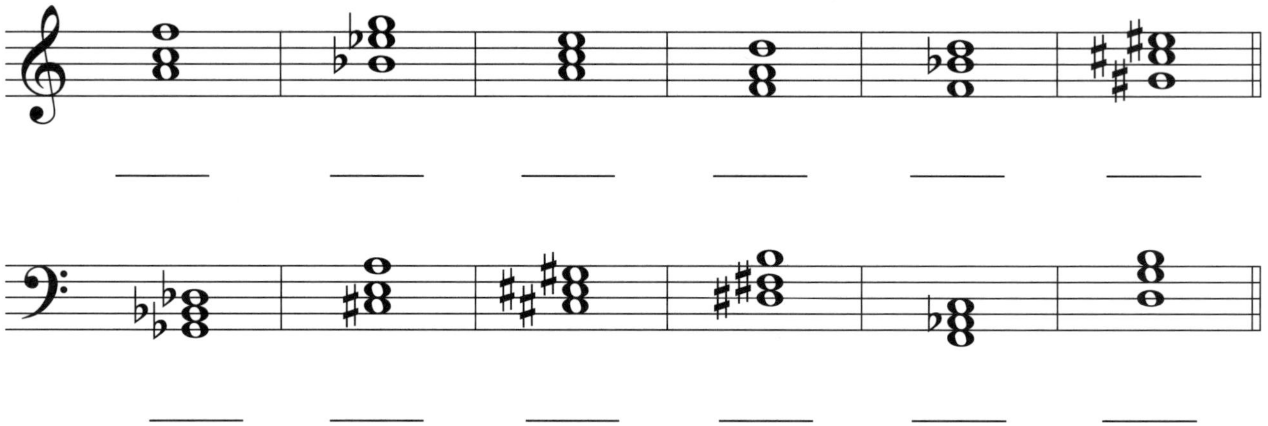

5. Using key signatures, write root position tonic, subdominant, and dominant triads in the following keys.

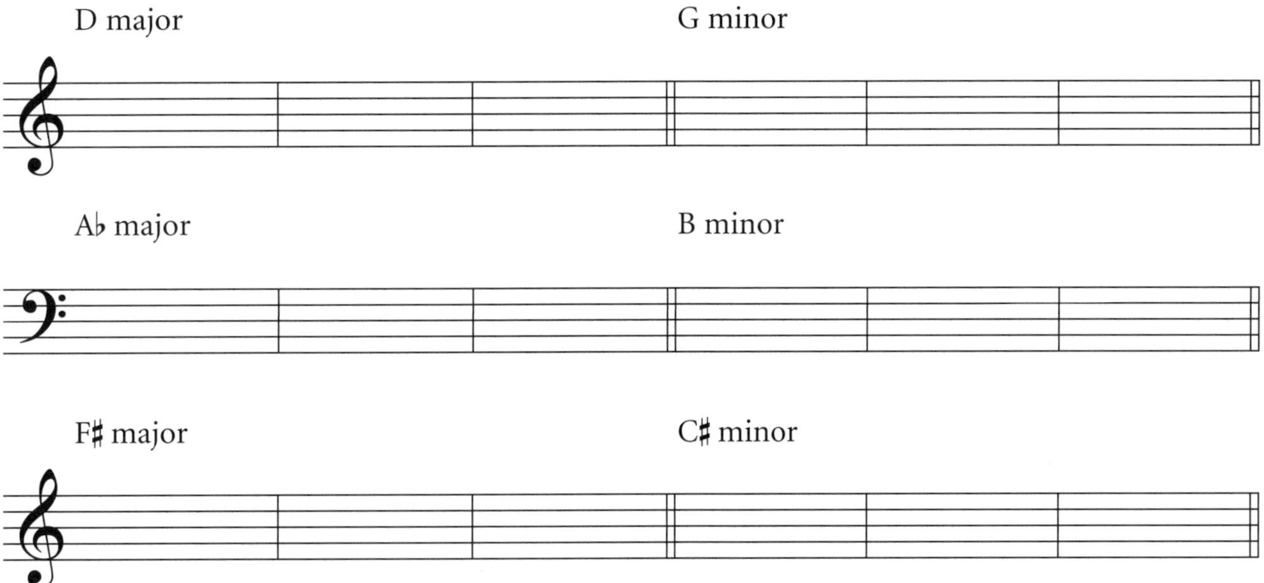

6. Name the root, type, and position of the following triads.

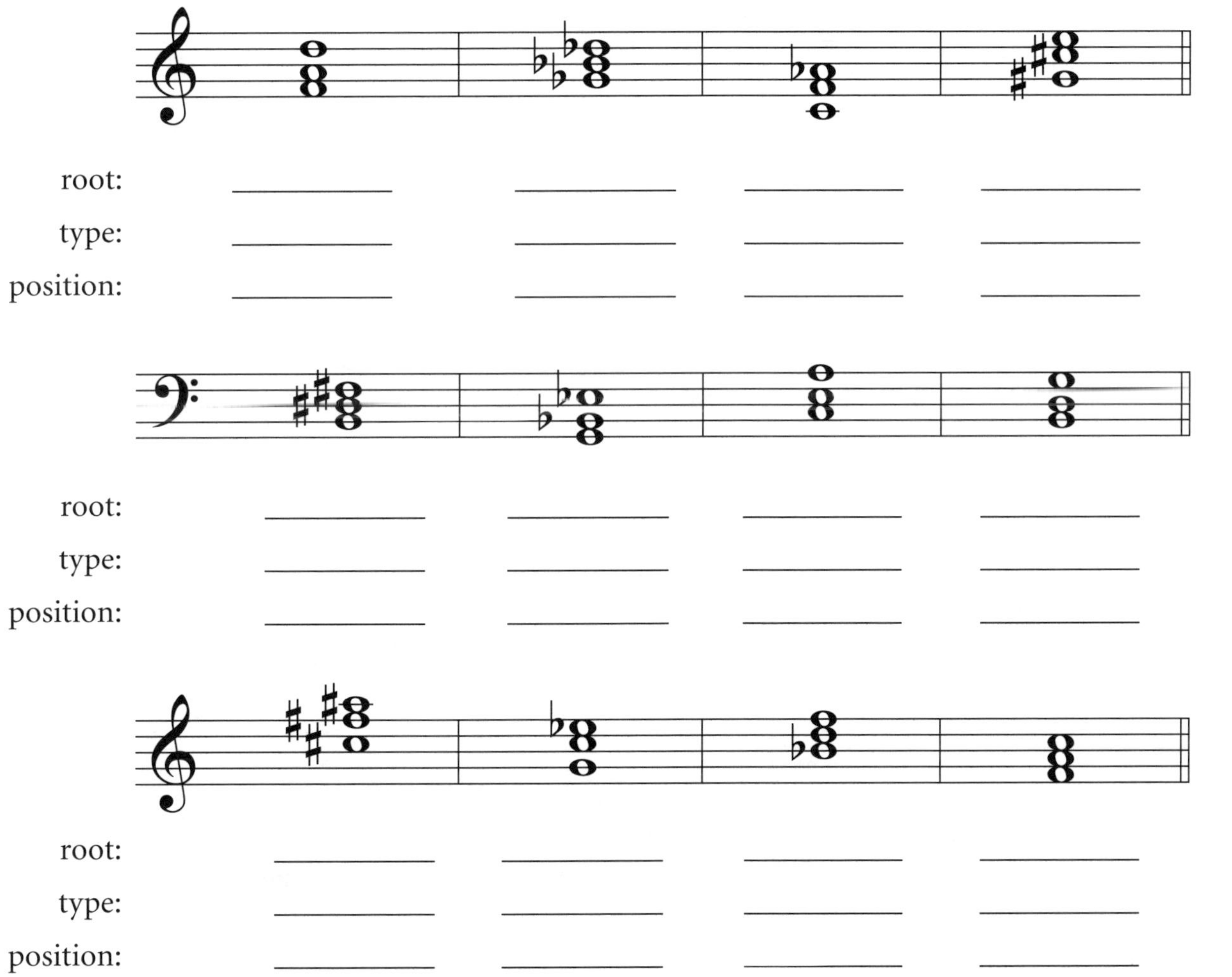

root: ___________ ___________ ___________ ___________

type: ___________ ___________ ___________ ___________

position: ___________ ___________ ___________ ___________

root: ___________ ___________ ___________ ___________

type: ___________ ___________ ___________ ___________

position: ___________ ___________ ___________ ___________

root: ___________ ___________ ___________ ___________

type: ___________ ___________ ___________ ___________

position: ___________ ___________ ___________ ___________

7. Write the following triads in first inversion, using the correct key signatures.

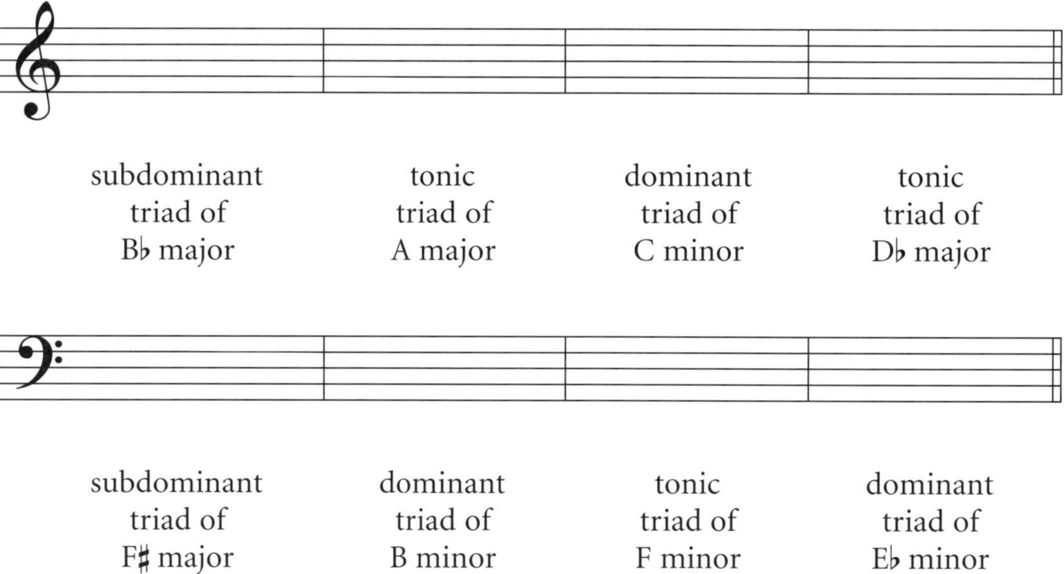

<table>
<tr><td>subdominant
triad of
B♭ major</td><td>tonic
triad of
A major</td><td>dominant
triad of
C minor</td><td>tonic
triad of
D♭ major</td></tr>
<tr><td>subdominant
triad of
F♯ major</td><td>dominant
triad of
B minor</td><td>tonic
triad of
F minor</td><td>dominant
triad of
E♭ minor</td></tr>
</table>

8. Write the following triads in root position, using accidentals instead of a key signature.

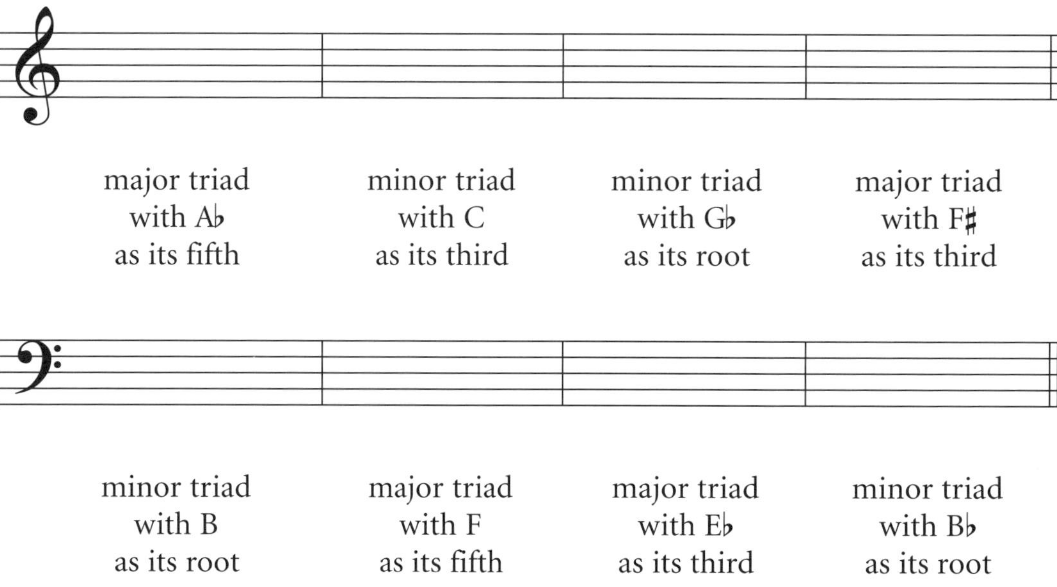

<table>
<tr><td>major triad
with A♭
as its fifth</td><td>minor triad
with C
as its third</td><td>minor triad
with G♭
as its root</td><td>major triad
with F♯
as its third</td></tr>
<tr><td>minor triad
with B
as its root</td><td>major triad
with F
as its fifth</td><td>major triad
with E♭
as its third</td><td>minor triad
with B♭
as its root</td></tr>
</table>

9. Write the following triads using accidentals instead of a key signature.

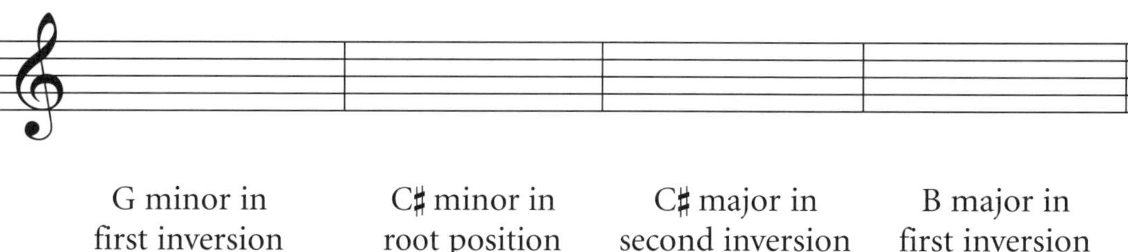

<table>
<tr><td>G minor in
first inversion</td><td>C♯ minor in
root position</td><td>C♯ major in
second inversion</td><td>B major in
first inversion</td></tr>
</table>

10. Name the root, type, and position of the following triads.

root: _______ _______ _______ _______ _______ _______

type: _______ _______ _______ _______ _______ _______

position: _______ _______ _______ _______ _______ _______

11. Learn the following Italian terms and their definitions.

rubato	a flexible tempo, using slight variations of speed to enhance musical expression
senza	without
tenuto	held, sustained
troppo	too much
una corda	one string, depress the left (piano) pedal
vivace	lively, brisk

CADENCES

A **cadence** is a place of rest in music. Cadences are two-chord progressions that occur at the ends of phrases and at the end of a piece of music. The **perfect cadence** is the most common cadence. It consists of the dominant triad moving to the tonic triad (V-I).

Cadences in the keyboard style are written with the root of each chord in the bass clef, and the root, third and fifth of each chord in the treble clef in close position.

A perfect cadence most often occurs over two measures, with the dominant chord on the last (or second last) beat of the first measure and the tonic chord on the first beat of the second measure.

Perfect Cadences in Major Keys

There are five steps for writing perfect cadences in keyboard style.

1. Write the key signature, and then write the roots of the dominant and tonic triads of that key in the bass clef. The dominant note may either rise a 4th or fall a 5th to the tonic note. Write the key and the chord progression below the bass staff using Roman numerals. (Note: you may also find it helpful to write the notes of each chord under the symbols.)

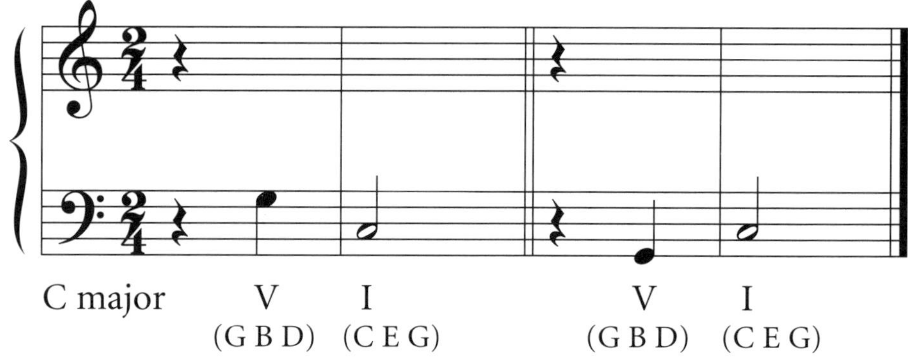

2. Write one of the notes of the dominant triad (root, third, or fifth) in the treble clef.

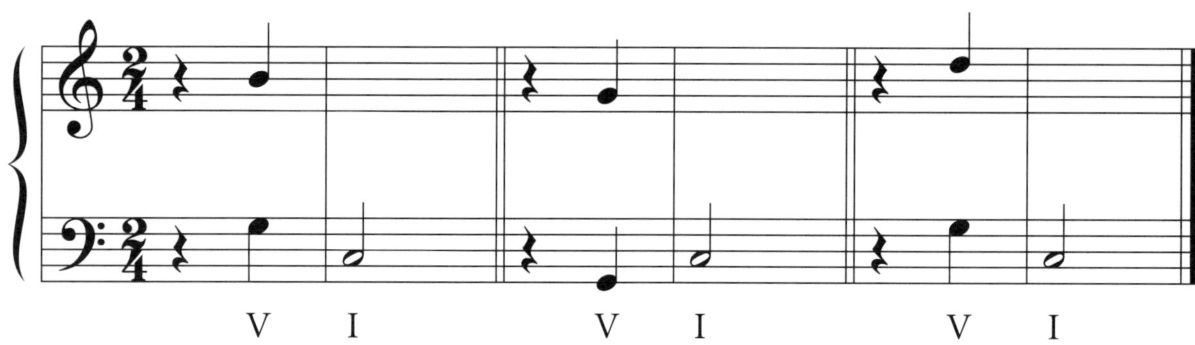

3. Complete the dominant triad by adding the remaining two notes under the treble note.

4. There is a common tone between the dominant and tonic triads. A common tone is a note that is the same in both chords. Copy that common tone above the tonic bass note at the same pitch.

5. Add the remaining two notes, keeping the shift from the dominant to the tonic chord as smooth as possible. Usually, these two notes move up one step.

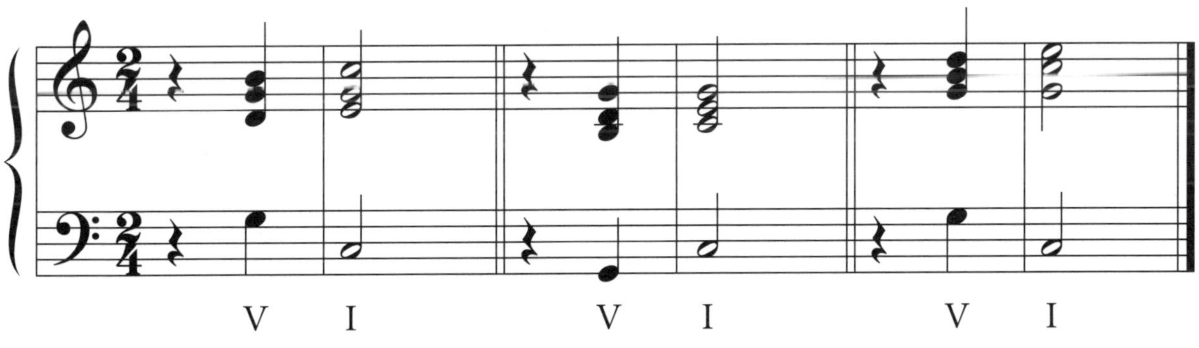

Perfect Cadences in Minor Keys

Perfect cadences in minor keys are much the same as those in major keys, but there are two important points.

1. The root is doubled in both the dominant and tonic chords.

2. In a minor key, the leading tone in the dominant chord must be raised. This means that the dominant chord will always have an accidental.

Study the following examples of perfect cadences.

1. Write two-measure examples of perfect cadences in the following keys, using key signatures.

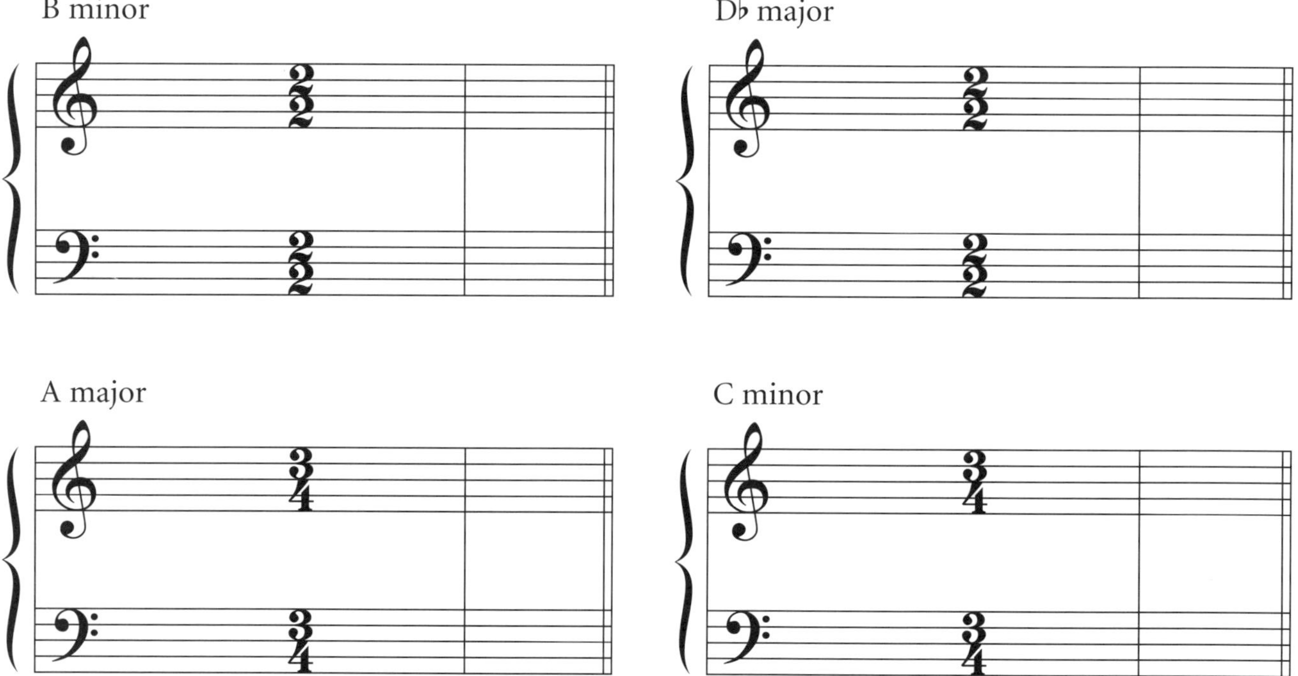

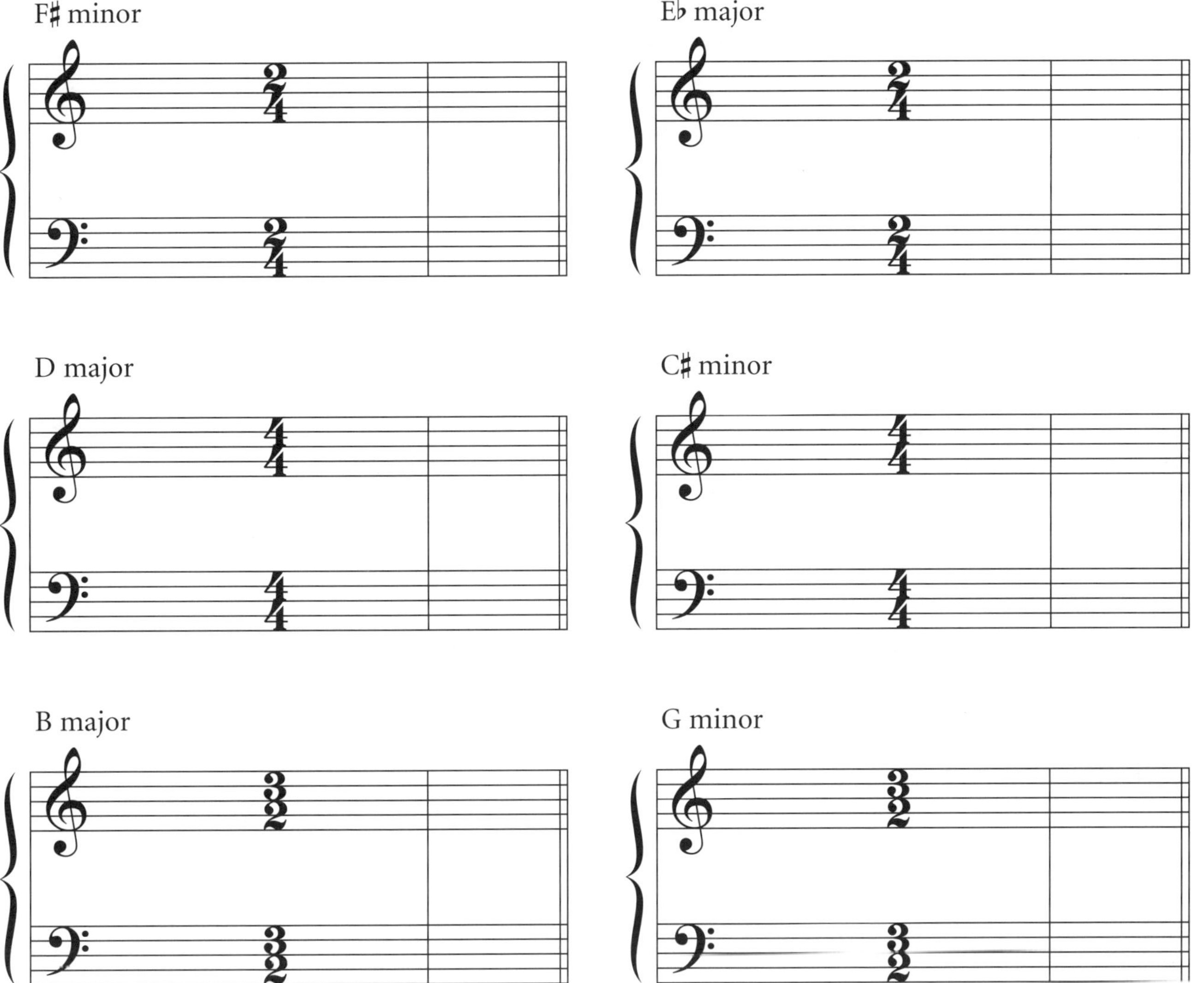

F# minor
Eb major
D major
C# minor
B major
G minor

Plagal Cadences

In a **plagal cadence,** the subdominant chord (IV) moves to the tonic chord (I). It most often occurs over two measures, with the subdominant chord on the last beat of the first measure and the tonic chord on the first beat of the second measure.

There are five steps for writing plagal cadences in keyboard style.

1. Write the key signature, and then write the roots of the subdominant and tonic triads of that key in the bass clef. The subdominant note may either rise a 5th or fall a 4th to the tonic note. Write the key and the chord progression below the bass staff using Roman numerals. (Note: you may also find it helpful to write the notes of each chord under the symbols.)

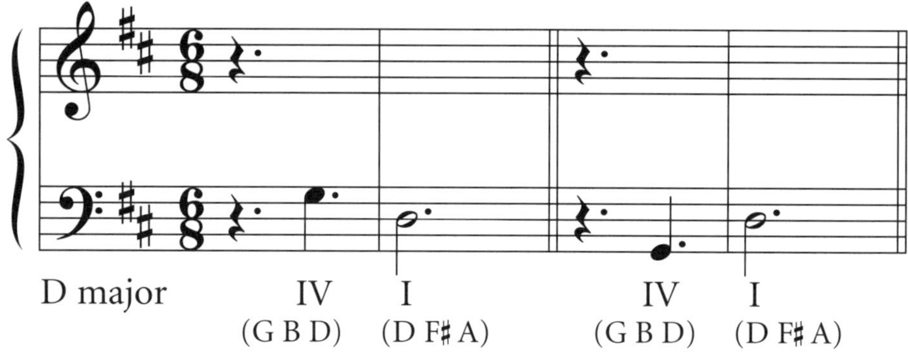

2. Write one of the notes of the subdominant triad (root, third, or fifth) in the treble clef.

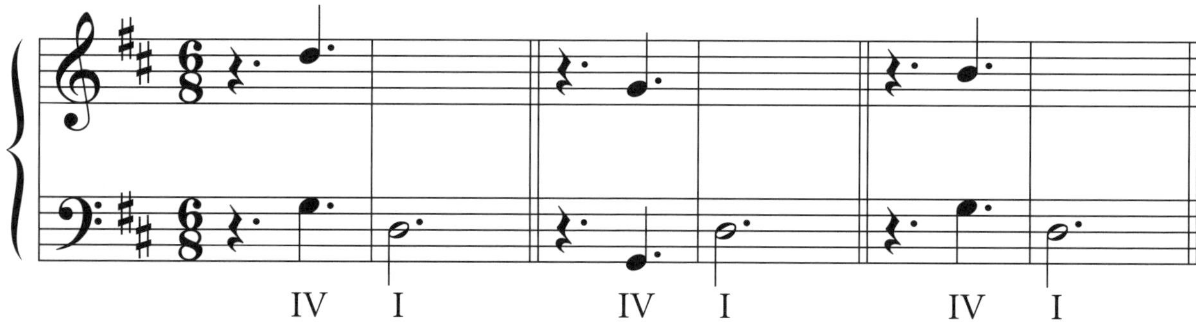

3. Complete the subdominant triad by adding the remaining two notes under the treble note.

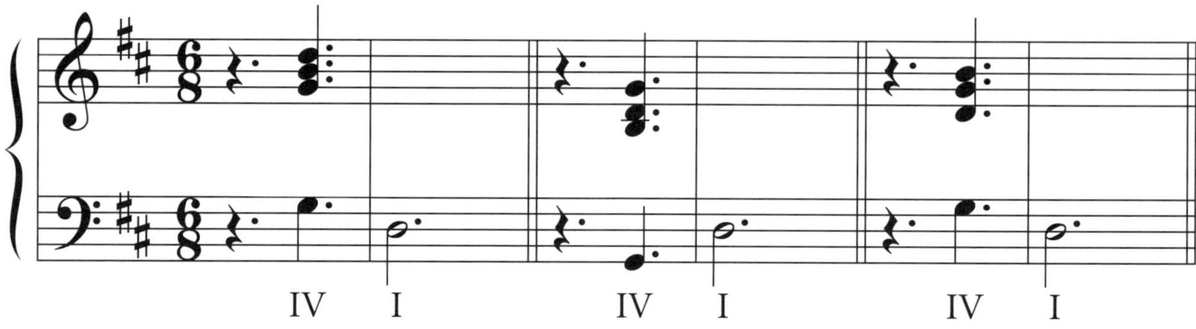

4. There is a common tone between the subdominant and tonic triads. Copy that common tone above the tonic bass note at the same pitch.

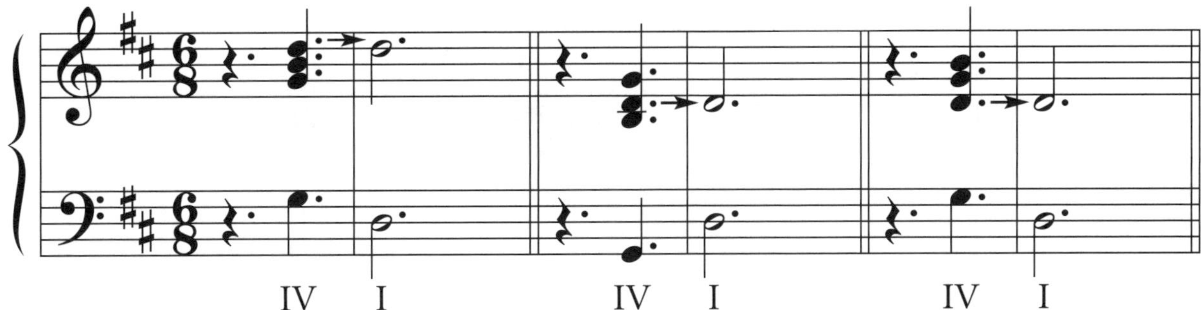

5. Add the remaining two notes of the tonic triad, keeping the shift from the subdominant to the tonic chord as smooth as possible. Usually, these two notes move down one step.

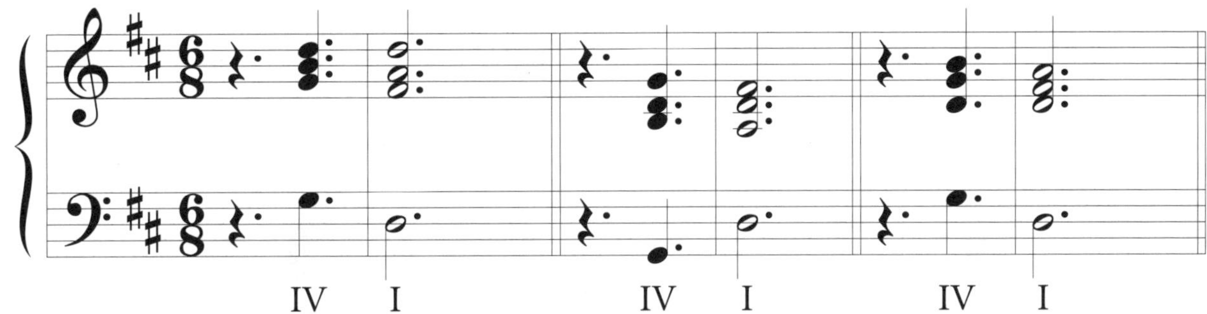

Study the following examples of plagal cadences.

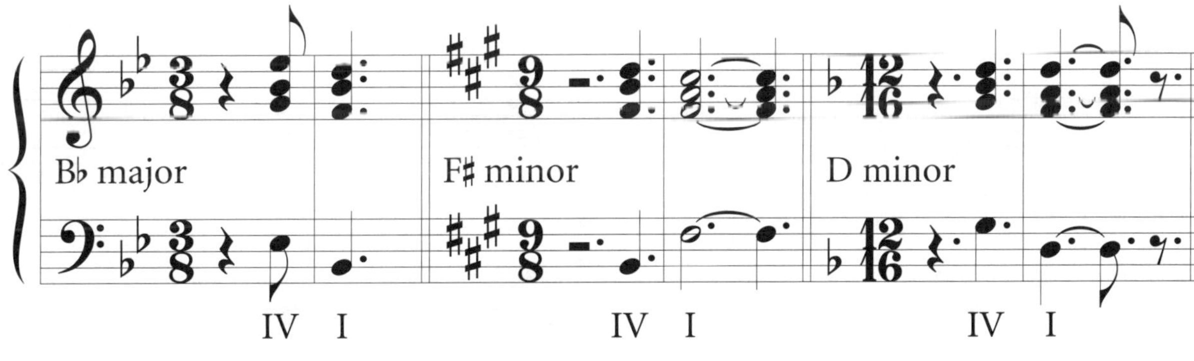

CADENCES

1. Write two-measure examples of plagal cadences in the following keys, using key signatures.

2. For the following chord progressions, name the key, name the cadence (perfect or plagal), and symbolize the chords (V-I or IV-I).

key: _____ _____ _____   cadence: _______________

key: _____ _____ _____   cadence: _______________

key: _____ _____ _____   cadence: _______________

key: _____ _____ _____   cadence: _______________

key: _____ _____ _____   cadence: _______________

key: _____ _____ _____   cadence: _______________

key: _____ _____ _____   cadence: _______________

key: _____ _____ _____   cadence: _______________

Cadences in Chorale Style

Cadences may be written in *chorale style*. A *chorale* is a hymn tune of the German Protestant church. Although some chorale tunes were written by composers, many others were adapted from Latin hymns or folk tunes. Composers also wrote four-part arrangements of chorale melodies. Some of the best known of these arrangements are by Johann Sebastian Bach.

In a chorale-style cadence, the chords are written in four parts, which are named for the four voices of a choir: *soprano, alto, tenor,* and *bass.* The soprano and alto voices are written in the treble clef, and the tenor and bass voices are written in the bass clef.

The example below shows four different positions of a C major chord written in chorale style.

This example demonstrates some of the rules for writing in chorale style.

1.   In each case, the root is doubled (that is, written twice).
2.   The stems of the soprano and tenor notes go up, and the stems of the alto and bass notes go down.
3.   The space between the soprano and alto voices, or between the alto and tenor voices, must not exceed one octave. The space between the tenor and bass voices can be up to twelve notes.

There are two points to remember about writing a perfect cadence in chorale style.

1.   Keep the common tone in the same voice.
2.   Move the other voices to the nearest available notes of the tonic chord.

In the following example, the root (G) of the dominant chord (V) is doubled. The common tone (G) stays in the alto. The bass drops a 5th to the root of the tonic chord (C), and the soprano and tenor rise one step.

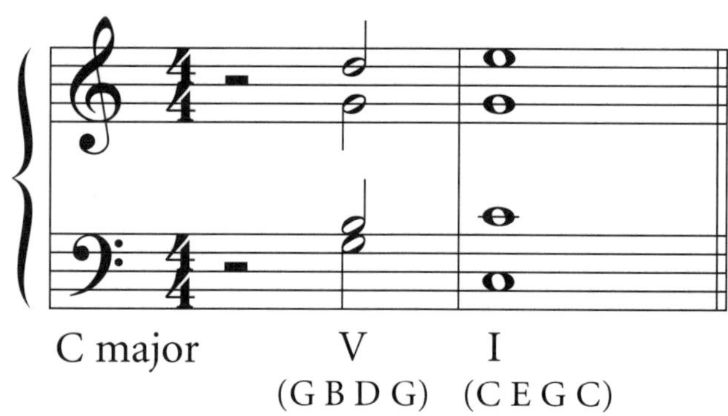

1. Fill in the missing voices below to create perfect cadences in chorale style.

    (a) Write the notes of each chord under the chord symbols.

    (b) Keep the common tone in the same voice.

    (c) Move the other voices to the nearest available note of the tonic chord.

    (d) Use an accidental to raise the leading tone (the third of chord V) in minor keys.

    (e) Do not put the soprano and alto, or the alto and tenor, more than one octave apart. (The interval between the bass and the tenor may be up to twelve notes.)

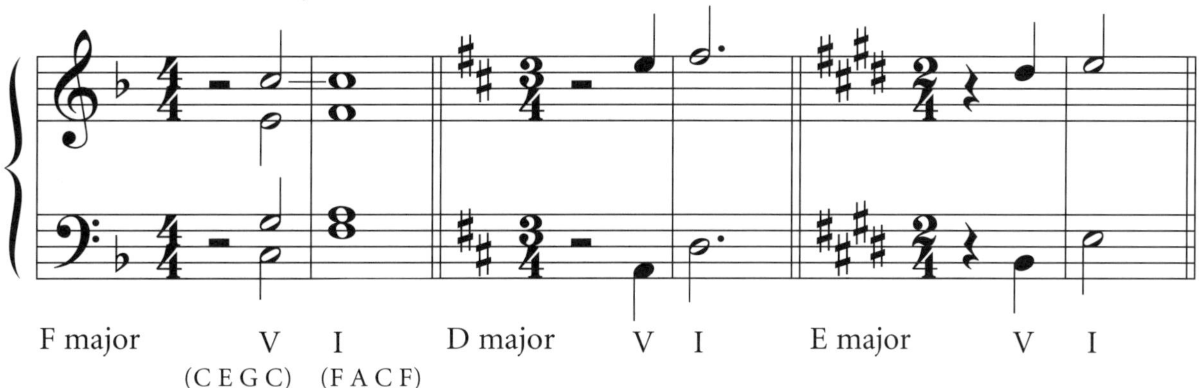

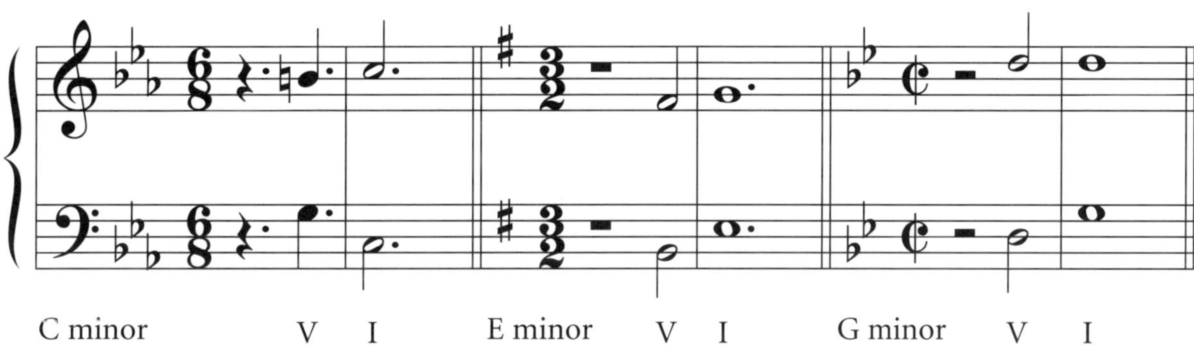

2. Add tonic chords to create perfect cadences in chorale style.

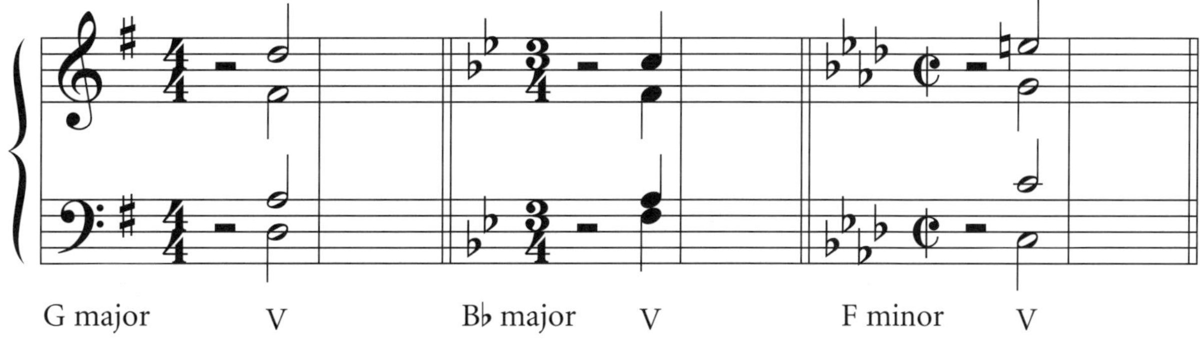

3.   Write perfect cadences in chorale style in the following keys.

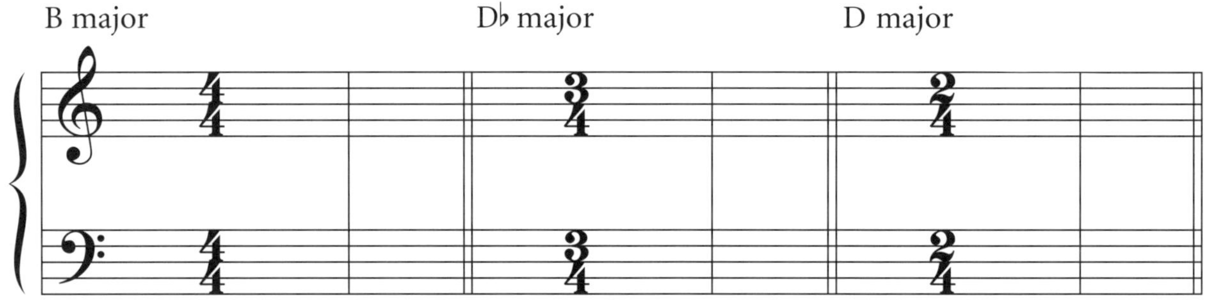

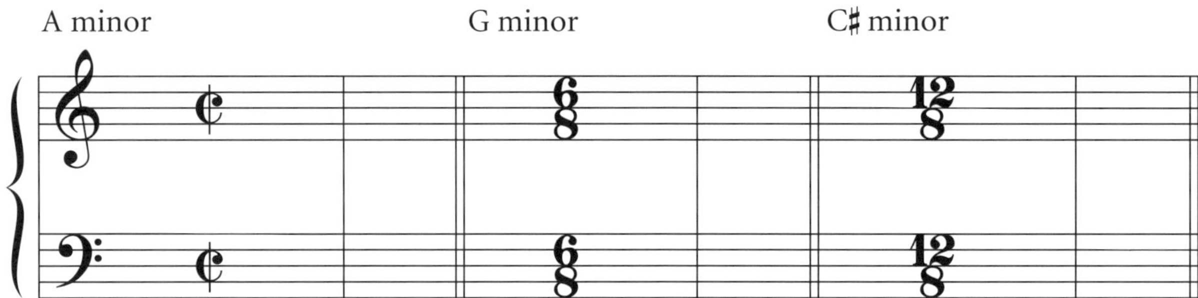

Plagal Cadences in Chorale Style

The same rules apply for writing plagal cadences in chorale style.

1.   Keep the common tone in the same voice.
2.   Move the other voices to the nearest available notes of the tonic chord.

In the example below, the root (F) of the subdominant (IV) chord is doubled. The common tone (C) stays in the tenor. The bass drops a 4th to the root of the tonic chord (C), and the soprano and alto fall one step.

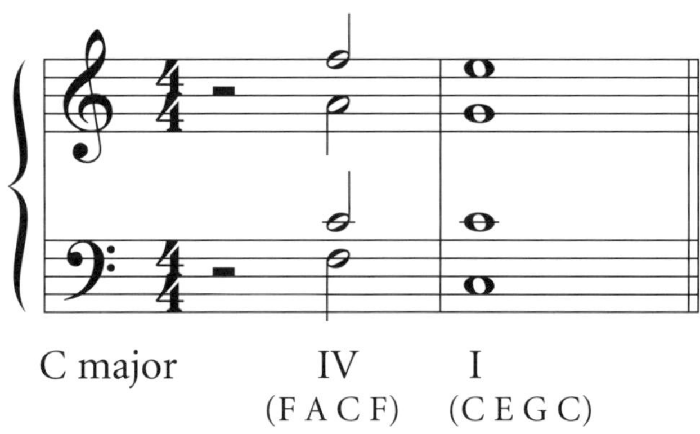

4. Fill in the soprano, alto, and tenor voices to create plagal cadences in chorale style.

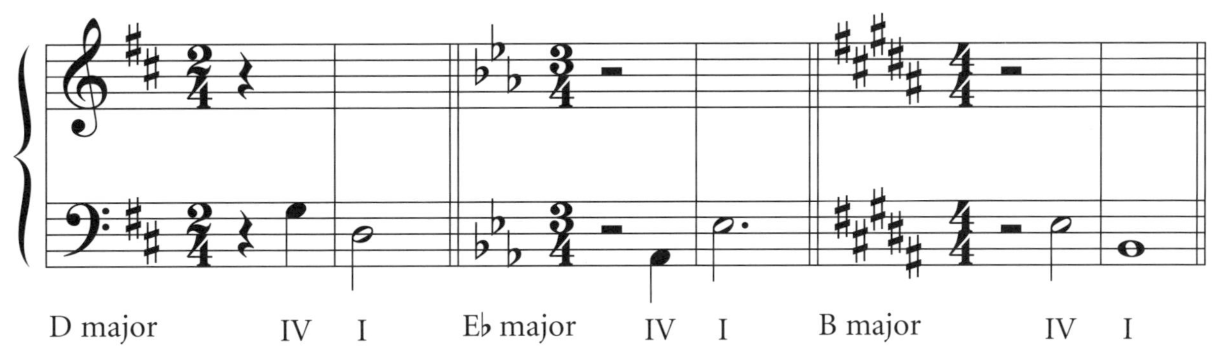

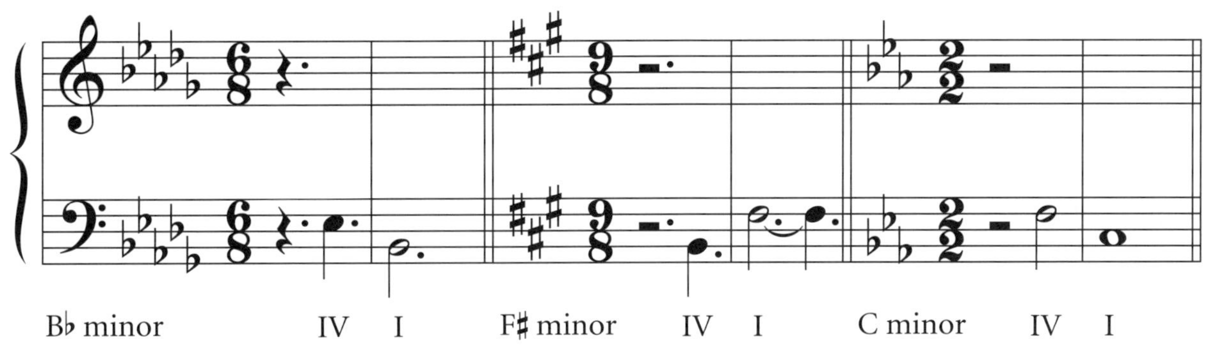

5. Write plagal cadences in chorale style in the following keys.

*R*EVIEW *3*

1. Write the following scales ascending and descending, using the correct key
    signature for each.

G♭ major in the treble clef, from mediant to mediant

A♭ melodic minor in the bass clef, from dominant to dominant

G♯ harmonic minor in the treble clef, from tonic to tonic

D♭ major in the bass clef, from leading note to leading note

F♯ major in the treble clef, from supertonic to supertonic

2. Name the root, type, and position of the following triads.

15

root: _______   _______   _______   _______   _______

type: _______   _______   _______   _______   _______

position: _______   _______   _______   _______   _______

3. Write the following triads using accidentals instead of a key signature.

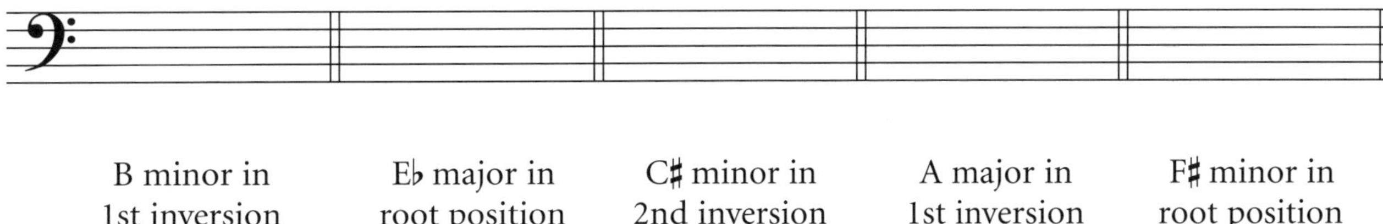

B minor in 1st inversion	E♭ major in root position	C♯ minor in 2nd inversion	A major in 1st inversion	F♯ minor in root position

4. Write the following two-measure cadences.

Plagal cadence in G major

Perfect cadence in D minor

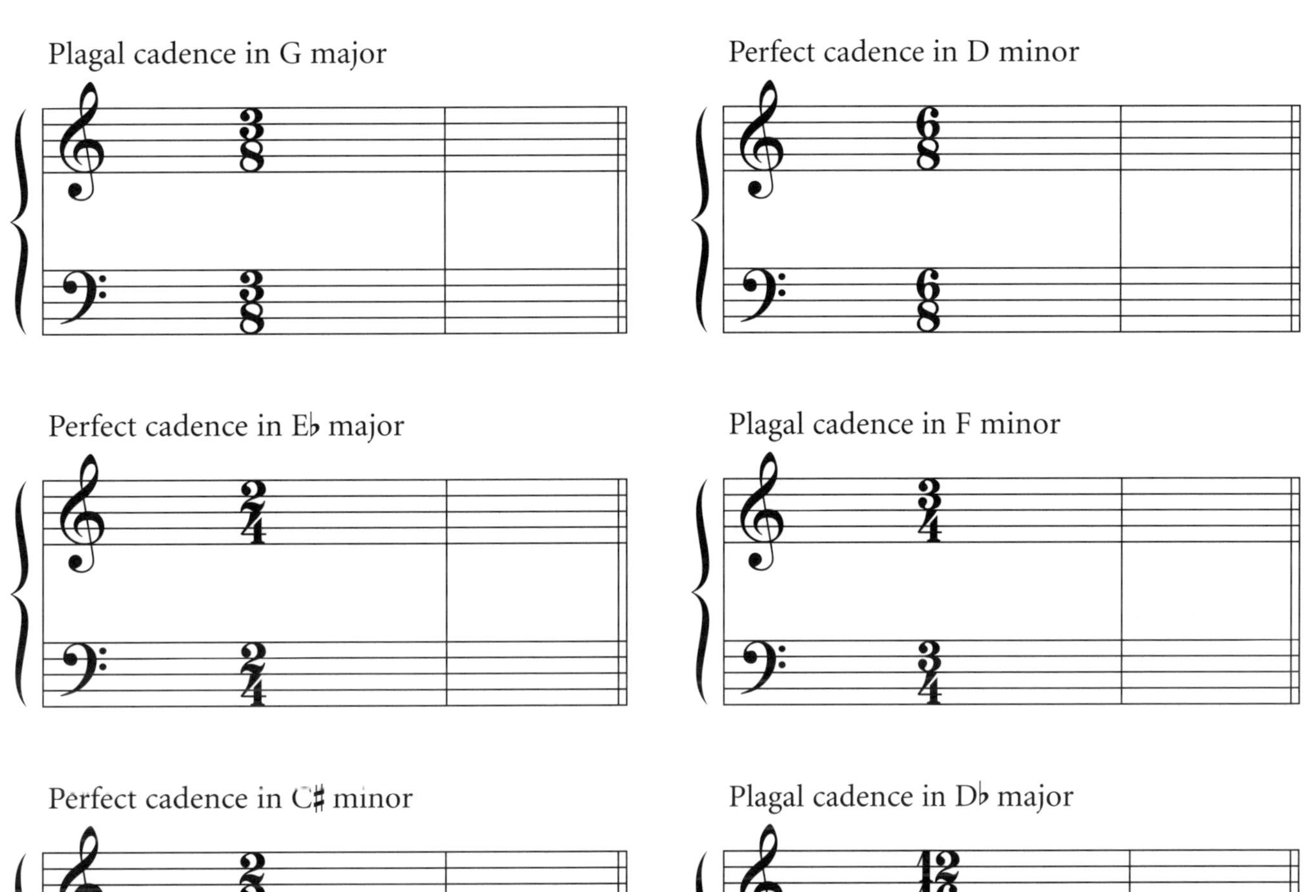

Perfect cadence in E♭ major

Plagal cadence in F minor

Perfect cadence in C♯ minor

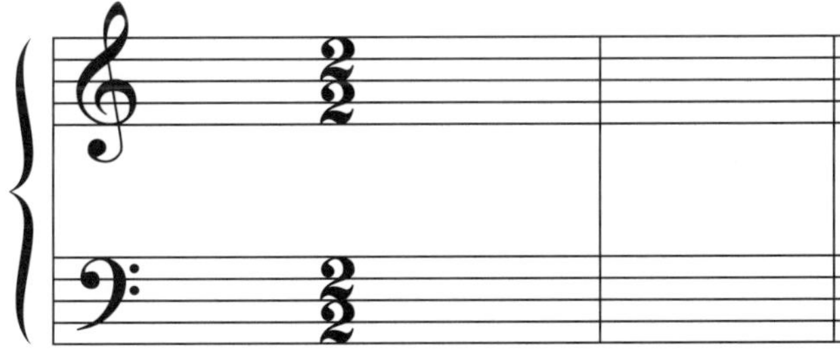

Plagal cadence in D♭ major

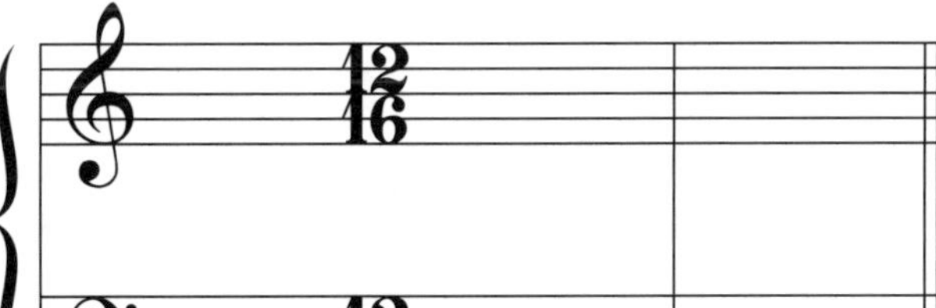

REVIEW 3

5. Match the following Italian terms with their definitions. (This list may contain terms from the Preliminary level list.)

<table>
<tr><td>_____ sempre</td><td>(a)</td><td>with movement</td></tr>
<tr><td>_____ più mosso</td><td>(b)</td><td>well</td></tr>
<tr><td>_____ poco</td><td>(c)</td><td>much, very much</td></tr>
<tr><td>_____ senza</td><td>(d)</td><td>one string, depress the left (piano) pedal</td></tr>
<tr><td>_____ vivace</td><td>(e)</td><td>always, continuously</td></tr>
<tr><td>_____ troppo</td><td>(f)</td><td>lively, brisk</td></tr>
<tr><td>_____ quasi</td><td>(g)</td><td>in the manner of</td></tr>
<tr><td>_____ tenuto</td><td>(h)</td><td>light, nimble, quick</td></tr>
<tr><td>_____ tempo</td><td>(i)</td><td>little by little</td></tr>
<tr><td>_____ poco a poco</td><td>(j)</td><td>held, sustained</td></tr>
<tr><td>_____ rubato</td><td>(k)</td><td>little</td></tr>
<tr><td>_____ ottava, 8va</td><td>(l)</td><td>a flexible tempo, using slight variations of speed to enhance musical expression</td></tr>
<tr><td>_____ Tempo primo</td><td>(m)</td><td>more movement (quicker)</td></tr>
<tr><td>_____ non troppo</td><td>(n)</td><td>return to the original tempo</td></tr>
<tr><td>_____ una corda</td><td>(o)</td><td>more</td></tr>
<tr><td>_____ non</td><td>(p)</td><td>speed at which music is performed</td></tr>
<tr><td>_____ più</td><td>(q)</td><td>quiet, tranquil</td></tr>
<tr><td>_____ assai</td><td>(r)</td><td>without</td></tr>
<tr><td>_____ ben</td><td>(s)</td><td>not too much</td></tr>
<tr><td>_____ con moto</td><td>(t)</td><td>not</td></tr>
<tr><td>_____ leggiero</td><td>(u)</td><td>the interval of an octave</td></tr>
<tr><td>_____ tranquillo</td><td>(v)</td><td>too much</td></tr>
</table>

FINDING THE KEY OF A MELODY

Accidentals

An accidental is a sign placed before a note to alter its pitch. Accidentals apply only to the note before which they are written. They do not alter the same note written an octave higher or lower.

An accidental lasts throughout a measure unless otherwise indicated. A bar line cancels an accidental except when the altered note is tied into the next measure. In this case, the tied note is the only note that is affected by the accidental.

Finding the Key of a Melody that has No Key Signature

The following melody contains a number of accidentals, but it has no key signature. How can we determine the key of this melody?

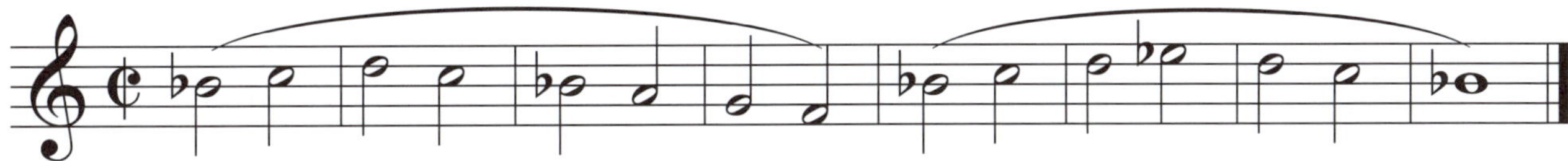

1. List the accidentals of the melody in the order in which they would appear in a key signature. This melody contains two flats: B flat and E flat.

2. Name the key signature. *Hints: If all the accidentals in the melody fit into a key signature, the melody is probably major. Often — but not always — a melody ends on the tonic note.*
   B flat and E flat are the first two flats in a key signature. The major key containing two flats is B flat major. Since there are no other accidentals, we can conclude that this melody is in B flat major. Another clue is that the melody ends on B flat.

Here is the melody written with a key signature:

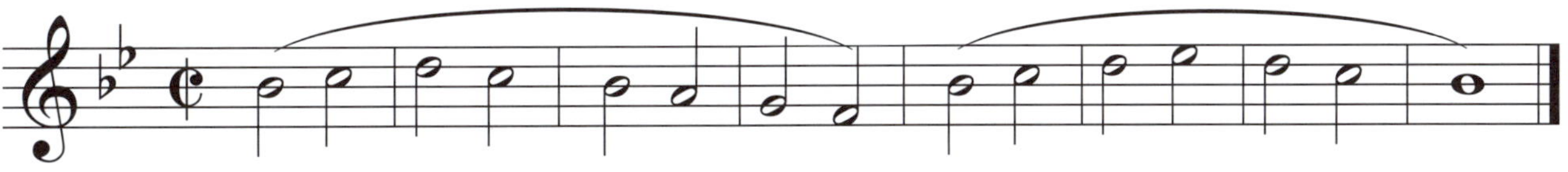

Finding the Key of a Melody

1. List the accidentals and name the keys of the following melodies. Rewrite the melodies using key signatures.

accidentals: ___________________

key: ___________________

accidentals: ___________________

key: ___________________

accidentals: ___________________

key: ___________________

Sometimes the accidentals in a melody do not form a recognizable key signature. If this is the case, there is a good chance that the melody is in a minor key.

1. This melody contains three flats: B flat, A flat, and D flat.

2. This could be the key signature of A flat major (four flats) but E flat is missing. The E in this melody could be the raised leading note of F minor. The key signature of F minor is four flats. (F minor is the relative minor of A flat major.) Another clue is that the melody begins and ends on F.

   Hint: If one note in a melody is raised, that note is often — but not always — the leading note of a minor key.

Here is the melody written with a key signature:

Here are two more examples:

1. This melody contains three sharps: F sharp, C sharp, and A sharp.

2. This could be the key signature of D major (two sharps) but we also have to explain the A sharp. The A sharp in this melody could be the raised leading note of B minor. The key signature of B minor is two sharps. (B minor is the relative minor of D major.) Another clue is that the melody ends on B.

1. This melody contains five sharps: F double sharp, C sharp, G sharp, D sharp, and A sharp.

2. This could be the key signature of B major (five sharps) but we also have to explain the F double sharp. F double sharp in this melody could be the raised leading note of G sharp minor. The key signature of G sharp minor is five sharps. (G sharp minor is the relative minor of B major.) Another clue is that the melody ends on G sharp.

FINDING THE KEY OF A MELODY

The last two examples on the previous page demonstrate two more helpful hints.

In minor key signatures of *up to four sharps,* there is always a skip of two sharps from the last sharp of the key signature to the leading tone. In minor melodies with key signatures of *five or more sharps,* the raised leading tone is always a double sharp.

There is another variation to watch for. In a minor key, the sixth degree (submediant) may also be raised. If both the sixth and seventh degrees of the scale are raised, this indicates the melodic form of the minor scale.

Remember that a melody may be in a minor key if:

1. The melody contains both sharps and flats.
2. The melody contains both sharps and double sharps.
3. The melody contains both flats and naturals.

2. List the accidentals and name the keys of the following melodies. Rewrite the melodies using key signatures.

accidentals: _______________________

key: _______________________

accidentals: _______________________

key: _______________________

Edvard Grieg
(1843–1907)
accidentals: _______________
key: _______________
Edward MacDowell
(1860–1908)
accidentals: _______________
key: _______________
accidentals: _______________
key: _______________
Pyotr Il'yich Tchaikovsky
(1840–1893)
accidentals: _______________
key: _______________

TRANSPOSITION

Transposition involves writing or playing music at a different pitch or in a different key. Here we will learn to transpose a melody from one major key to another major key.

To transpose a melody into a new key, you must know the original key of the melody and either the new key or the interval of transposition. If the interval of transposition is given, you must determine the new key.

Here is a melody in G major.

To transpose this melody up a major 3rd, follow these four steps.

1. Determine the original key. The original key is G major.

2. Find the note that is a major 3rd above G. This note will be the tonic of the new key. A major 3rd above G is B. The new key will be B major.

3. Write the key signature of the new key. B major has a key signature of five sharps.

4. Move each note in the original melody up a 3rd. (Note that because we have used the key signature of the new key, every one of these 3rds will be a major 3rd.)

Here is the melody transposed into B major.

If a melody contains accidentals, the transposed melody will also contain accidentals. If a note in the original melody is raised, the corresponding transposed note must be raised. If a note in the original melody is lowered, the corresponding transposed note must be lowered.

In the following example, the original melody in B flat major has been transposed up a major 2nd to C major. The original melody contains two accidentals: E natural (measure 2) and B natural (measure 3). Both these notes have been raised one semitone.

This means that the corresponding notes in the transposed melody (F and C) must also be raised one semitone: F sharp (measure 2) and C sharp (measure 3).

1. Name the key of the following melody.
   (a) Transpose it up a perfect 4th and name the new key.
   (b) Transpose it up a minor 3rd and name the new key.

key: ___________

(a)

key: ___________

(b)

key: ___________

2. Name the key of the following melody.

   (a) Transpose it up a major 2nd and name the new key.

   (b) Transpose it into the key of F♯ major.

key: _________

(a)

key: _________

(b)

3. Name the key of the following melody.

   (a) Transpose it into the key of B major.

   (b) Transpose it up a major 3rd and name the new key.

key: _________

(a)

(b)

key: _________

4. Name the key of the following melody.
   (a) Transpose it up a perfect 5th and name the new key.
   (b) Transpose it up a major 2nd and name the new key.

key: _____________

(a)

key: _____________

(b)

key: _____________

5. Name the key of the following melody.
   (a) Transpose it into the key of D♭ major.
   (b) Transpose it up a minor 6th and name the new key.

key: _____________

(a)

(b)

key: _____________

Transposition

6. Name the key of the following melody.
    (a) Transpose it up a perfect 4th and name the new key.
    (b) Transpose it into the key of A major

key: ___________

(a)

key: ___________

(b)

7. Learn the following Italian terms and their definitions.

e, ed	and
*fortepiano, **fp***	loud then suddenly soft
grave	slow and solemn
loco	return to the normal register
ma	but
meno	less
meno mosso	less movement, slower
M.M.	metronome marking (Maelzel's Metronome)
molto	much, very

REVIEW 4

100

30

1. Name the keys of the following melodies. Rewrite them using key signatures.

2. Name the key of the following melody.

40

    (a) Transpose it up a major 3rd and name the new key.

    (b) Transpose it up a perfect 4th and name the new key.

    (c) Transpose it up a perfect 5th and name the new key.

    (d) Transpose it into the key of A major.

Edvard Grieg
(1843–1907)

key: __________

(a)

key: __________

(b)

key: __________

(c)

key: __________

(d)

3. Match the following Italian terms with their definitions.

30

____ *molto*	(a) without
____ *grave*	(b) almost, as if
____ *fortepiano*	(c) much, very
____ *e, ed*	(d) metronome marking (Maelzel's Metronome)
____ *loco*	(e) less movement, slower
____ *ma*	(f) lively, brisk
____ *meno*	(g) held, sustained
____ M.M.	(h) expressive, with expression
____ *meno mosso*	(i) return to normal register
____ *vivace*	(j) and
____ *tenuto*	(k) less
____ *quasi*	(l) slow and solemn
____ *ben*	(m) but
____ *espressivo*	(n) well
____ *senza*	(o) loud then suddenly soft

Music Analysis

1. Analyze the following music by answering the questions below.

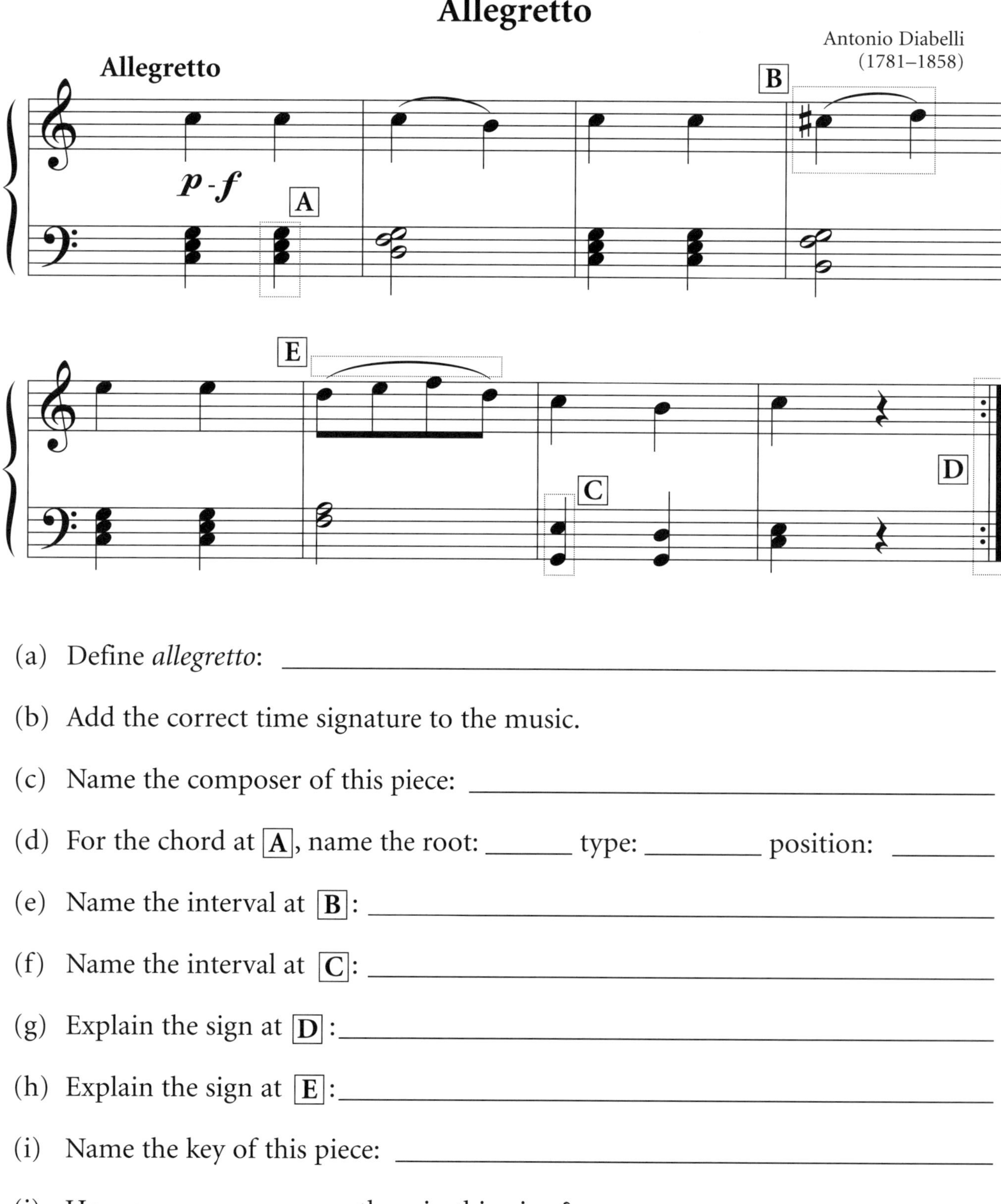

(a) Define *allegretto*: ____

(b) Add the correct time signature to the music.

(c) Name the composer of this piece: _______________________________________

(d) For the chord at [A], name the root: _______ type: _________ position: _______

(e) Name the interval at [B]: _______________________________________

(f) Name the interval at [C]: _______________________________________

(g) Explain the sign at [D]: _______________________________________

(h) Explain the sign at [E]: _______________________________________

(i) Name the key of this piece: _______________________________________

(j) How many measures are there in this piece? _______________________________

Broken Chord Accompaniment

Often a piece of music often has an accompaniment based on broken chords.

If you put the notes together, using the lowest note as a reference point, you can find the root, position and type of chord in the accompaniment.

The examples below are broken-triad accompaniments.

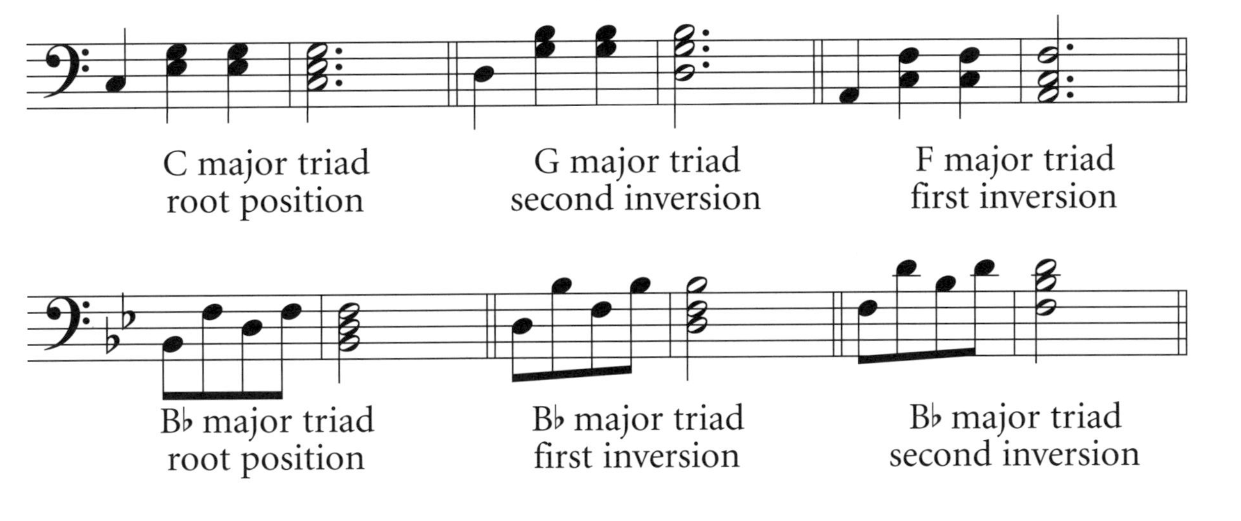

2. Name the root, type, and position of the broken chords in the following example.

Little Waltz

3. Analyze the following music by answering the questions below.

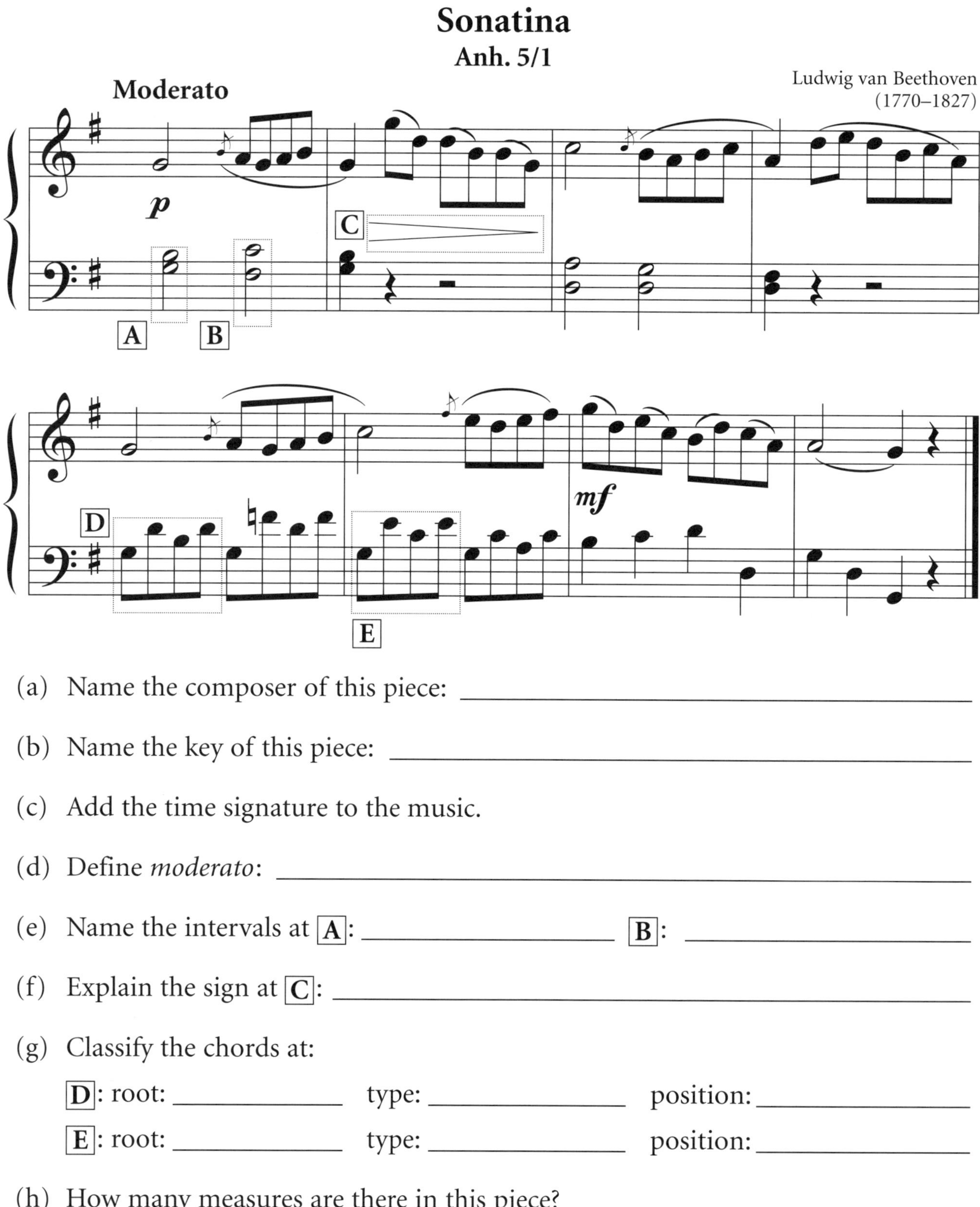

(a) Name the composer of this piece: _______________________________________

(b) Name the key of this piece: _______________________________________

(c) Add the time signature to the music.

(d) Define *moderato*: _______________________________________

(e) Name the intervals at A: _________________ B: _________________

(f) Explain the sign at C: _______________________________________

(g) Classify the chords at:

D: root: ___________ type: ___________ position: ___________

E: root: ___________ type: ___________ position: ___________

(h) How many measures are there in this piece? _______________________

4. Analyze the following music by answering the questions below.

Source: *First Instruction in Playing Playing: One Hundred Recreations,* no. 28

(a) Name the composer of this piece: _________________________________

(b) Define *allegro:* _________________________________

(c) Explain the sign at A: _________________________________

(d) Name the chords at:

B: root: ___________ type: _____________ position: ___________
C: root: ___________ type: _____________ position: ___________

(e) How many measures are there in this piece? _________________________

(f) Add the time signature to the music.

(g) Name the intervals at letter D: _________ E: _________ F: _________

(h) Explain the sign at G: _________________________________

5. Analyze the following music by answering the questions below.

(a) Name the composer of this piece: _______________________________________

(b) When did this composer live? _______________________________________

(c) Name the key of this piece:_______________________________________

(d) Classify the chords at:

    A : root: ___________   type: _____________   position:_______________

    B : root: ___________   type: _____________   position:_______________

    C : root: ___________   type: _____________   position:_______________

    D : root: ___________   type: _____________   position:_______________

    E : root: ___________   type: _____________   position:_______________

(e) Add the time signature to the music.

(f) Explain the sign at F : _______________________________________

(g) Explain the sign at G : _______________________________________

(h) Explain the sign at H : _______________________________________

Music Terms and Signs

accelerando	becoming quicker
alla, all'	in the manner of
animato	lively, animated
assai	much, very much (for example, *allegro assai*: very fast)
ben, bene	well (for example, *ben marcato*: well marked)
blues scale	a major scale in which the 3rd, the 7th, and sometimes the 5th degrees are lowered
col, coll', colla, colle	with (for example, *coll'ottava*: with an added octave)
con	with
con brio	with vigor or spirit
con espressione	with expression
con moto	with movement
e, ed	and
espressivo	expressive, with expression
fortepiano, **fp**	loud, then suddenly soft
grave	slow and solemn
leggiero	light, nimble, quick
loco	return to normal register
ma	but (for example, *ma non troppo*: but not too much)
meno	less
meno mosso	less movement, slower
M.M.	metronome marking
molto	much, very
non	not
non troppo	not too much
octatonic scale	an eight-note scale consisting of a strict alternation of tones and semitones

pentatonic scale	a five-note scale (one example is found on the black keys of the keyboard)
più	more
più mosso	more movement, quicker
poco	little
poco a poco	little by little
quasi	almost, as if
rubato	a flexible tempo using slight variations of speed to enhance musical expression
sempre	always, continuously
senza	without
tenuto	held, sustained
tranquillo	quiet, tranquil
tre corde	three strings: release the left piano pedal
troppo	too much
una corda	one string: depress the left piano pedal
vivace	lively, brisk

Practice Test

1. Name the following intervals.

5

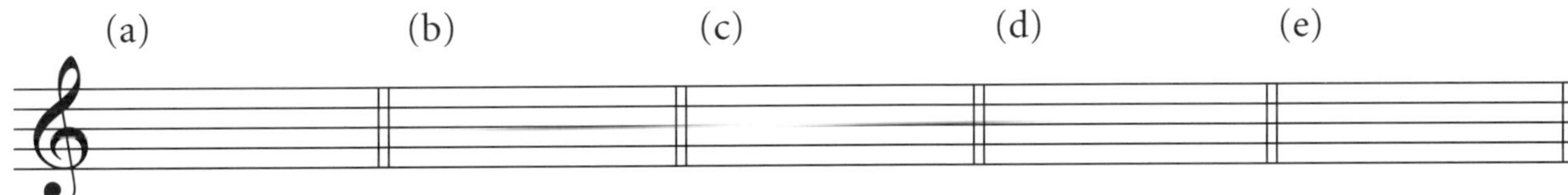

2. Invert the above intervals and rename them.

5

3. Write the following triads using a key signature for each.

10

   (a)   the tonic triad of B♭ major
   (b)   the dominant triad of C♯ minor
   (c)   the subdominant triad of D♭ major
   (d)   the tonic triad of F♯ major
   (e)   the dominant triad of A♭ minor

   (a)   (b)   (c)   (d)   (e)

4. Define the following Italian terms.

10

accelerando ____

Tempo primo ____

grave ____

prestissimo ____

*dolce*____

10   5.   Write the following scales in the treble clef, ascending and descending, from tonic to tonic, using key signatures.

     (a)   the major scale with D♯ as the supertonic

     (b)   the harmonic minor scale with G as the dominant

     (c)   the melodic minor scale with G♭ as the mediant

(a)

(b)

(c)

10   6.   Name the key of the following melody. Transpose it up a minor 6th, and name the new key.

Franz Schubert
(1797–1828)

key: _____________

key: _____________

10
7. Add rests under the brackets to complete the following one-measure rhythms.

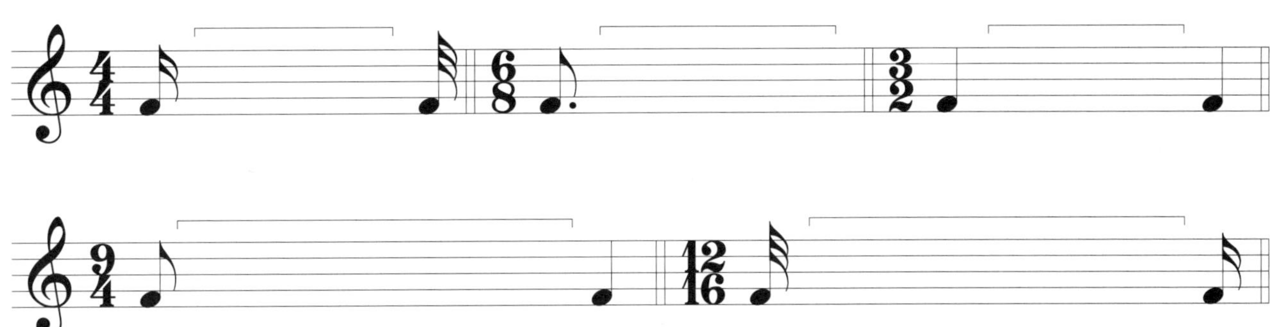

10
8. Add time signatures to the following one-measure rhythms.

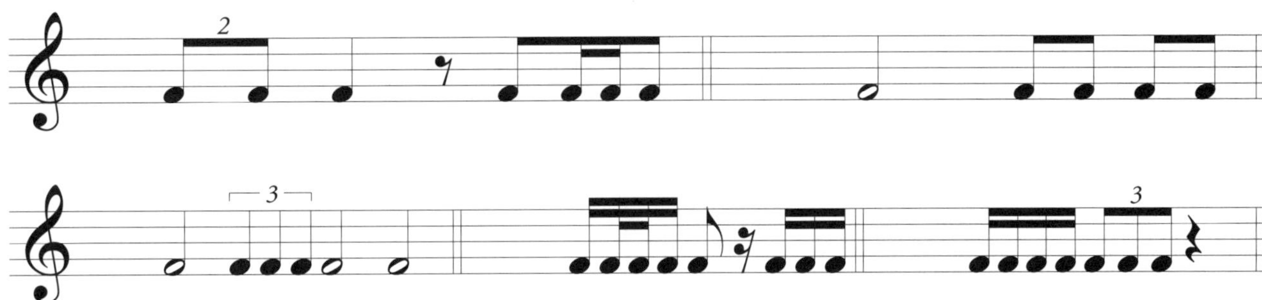

10
9. Write the following cadences in keyboard style using key signatures.
   (a) a perfect cadence in D minor
   (b) a plagal cadence in B major

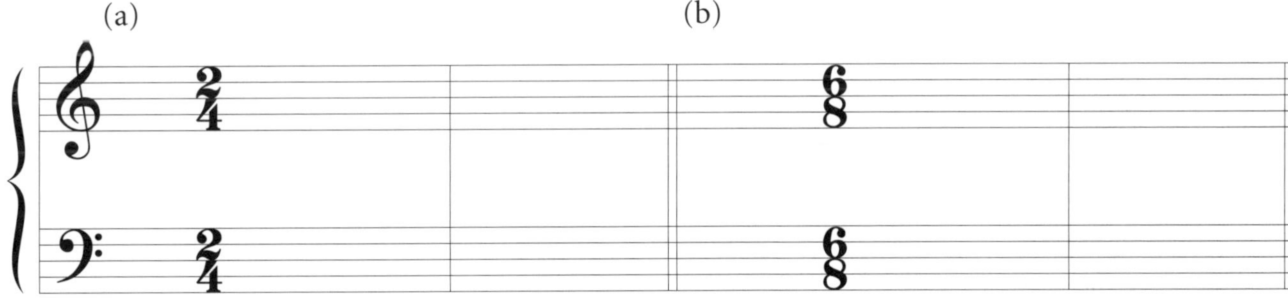

10. (a) Name the minor key for each key signature.
    (b) Name the degree of the scale for each note.

(a)________ ________   ________ ________ ________

(b)________ ________   ________ ________ ________

11. Rewrite the following melodies, omitting the accidentals and using key signatures. Name the key of each melody.

key: __________

key: __________

GRADE

60–69 (Pass)   70–79 (Honors)   80–89 (First Class Honors)   90–100 (Distinction)

GLOSSARY

accidental	a symbol, placed in front of a note, that raises or lowers its pitch
augmented interval	an interval that is one chromatic semitone larger than the equivalent major or perfect interval
bar line	a vertical line that divides the staff into measures
bass clef 𝄢	the clef that indicates the location of F on the fourth line of the staff
beam	a horizontal line that connects two or more eighth, sixteenth, or thirty-second notes
blues scale	a major scale in which the 3rd, the 7th, and sometimes the 5th degrees are lowered
cadence	two chords or implied harmonies that end a phrase of music, creating a place of rest
chorale style	a style of written music for four distinct voices: soprano, alto, tenor, and bass
chord	a combination of notes that are played together
chromatic semitone	a semitone that consists of two notes with the same letter name (for example, G – G$\sharp$)
circle of fifths	a diagram that shows how keys are related by perfect fifths
clef	the sign placed at the beginning of a staff to indicate the location of notes
common time $\mathbf{C}$	another name for the time signature $\frac{4}{4}$
compound duple time	time signatures that indicate two beats in each measure — for example, $\frac{6}{4}$, $\frac{6}{8}$, $\frac{6}{16}$ — where each beat is divisible by three
compound quadruple time	time signatures that indicate four beats in each measure — for example, $\frac{12}{4}$, $\frac{12}{8}$, $\frac{12}{16}$ — where each beat is divisible by three
compound time	time signatures in which each beat is divisible by three
compound triple time	time signatures that indicate three beats in each measure — for example, $\frac{9}{4}$, $\frac{9}{8}$, $\frac{9}{16}$ — where each beat is divisible by three
cut time (*alla breve*) $\mathcal{C}$	another name for the time signature $\frac{2}{2}$

diatonic semitone	a semitone that consists of two notes with different letter names (for example, G – A♭)
diminished interval	an interval that is one chromatic semitone smaller than the equivalent a minor or perfect interval
double flat ♭♭	the sign that lowers the pitch of a note one whole tone
double sharp ✕	the sign that raises the pitch of a note one whole tone
double whole note, breve ‖o‖	in $\frac{4}{2}$ time, a note equal to four beats
duplet	in compound time, a group of two notes that are played in the time of three notes of the same value
enharmonic	describes notes of the same pitch that are named differently (for example, F♯ and G♭, or D♯ and E♭)
fifth	in a chord, the note that is the interval of a 5th above the root
first inversion	the position of a chord when the third is the lowest note
flag	a small curved line that, when attached to a note stem, indicates an eighth note (two flags indicate a sixteenth note; three indicate a thirty-second note)
flat ♭	the sign that lowers the pitch of a note one semitone
grand staff	the combination of the treble and bass staves
harmonic interval	the distance between two notes played at the same time
harmonic minor scale	a scale formed by raising the seventh degree of the natural minor scale (There are semitones between notes two and three, notes five and six, and notes seven and eight.)
interval	the distance between two notes
inverted	turned upside down
key	the specific scale on which a piece of music is based
key signature	a collection of sharps or flats at the beginning of the staff that indicates the key of the music
ledger lines	the short lines used for notes that are above or below the staff

major interval (maj)	the interval of a 2nd, 3rd, 6th, or 7th, as formed above the tonic of a major scale
major scale	a series of seven notes with the following pattern of tones and semitones: tone – tone – semitone – tone – tone – tone – semitone
major triad	a three-note chord that consists of a major 3rd and a perfect 5th above the root
measure	a group of beats or pulses between two bar lines
melodic interval	the distance between two notes played one after the other
melodic minor scale	a scale formed by raising the sixth and seventh degrees of the natural minor scale ascending, and lowering the sixth and seventh degrees descending (There are semitones between notes two and three and notes seven and eight ascending, and between notes six and five and notes three and two descending.)
minor interval (min)	the interval of a 2nd, 3rd, 6th, or 7th that is one semitone smaller than the equivalent major interval
minor scale	*see* **natural minor scale, harmonic minor scale,** and **melodic minor scale**
minor triad	a three-note chord that consists of a minor 3rd and a perfect 5th above the root
natural ♮	the sign that cancels a sharp or a flat
natural minor scale	a minor scale written with no changes from the key signature (There are semitones between notes two and three and notes five and six.)
note	a written symbol used to indicate sound in music
octatonic scale	an eight-note scale in which tones and semitones alternate
pentatonic scale	a five-note scale (one example is found on the black keys of the keyboard)
perfect cadence	a chord progression that consists of a dominant triad moving to a tonic triad (V-I)
perfect interval (per)	an interval of a unison, 4th, 5th, or 8ve as formed above the tonic of a major scale
plagal cadence	a chord progression that consists of a subdominant triad moving to a tonic triad (IV-I)

GLOSSARY

quadruplet	in compound time, a group of four notes that are played in the time of three notes of the same value
quintuplet	a group of five notes that are played in the time of three, four, or six notes of the same value, depending on the time signature
relative keys	major and minor keys that use the same key signature (The relative minor of a major key is three semitones lower: for example, the relative minor of D major is B minor.)
rest	a written symbol used to indicate silence in music
root	the fundamental note of a triad or chord
root position	the position of a chord when the root is the lowest note
scale	a series of notes with a specific pattern of tones and semitones
second inversion	the position of a chord when the fifth is the lowest note
semitone	one half step; the shortest distance between two notes on the keyboard
septuplet	a group of seven notes that are played in the time of four or six notes of the same value
sextuplet	a group of six notes that are played in the time of four notes of the same value
sharp ♯	the sign that raises the pitch of a note one semitone
short score	a score for four voices (soprano, alto, tenor, and bass) written on two staves
simple duple time	time signatures that indicate two beats in each measure — for example, $\frac{2}{2}$, $\frac{2}{4}$, $\frac{2}{8}$ — where each beat is divisible by two
simple quadruple time	time signatures that indicate four beats in each measure — for example, $\frac{4}{2}$, $\frac{4}{4}$, $\frac{4}{8}$ — where each beat is divisible by two
simple time	time signatures in which each beat is divisible by two
simple triple time	time signatures that indicate three beats in each measure — for example, $\frac{3}{2}$, $\frac{3}{4}$, $\frac{3}{8}$ — where each beat is divisible by two
staff (*pl.* staves)	the five horizontal lines on and between which notes are written
syncopation	a shift of accent from a strong beat to a weak beat

third	in a chord, the note that is a 3rd above the root
tie	a curved line that connects two notes of the same pitch (The first note is played and the sound is held for the value of both notes.)
time signature	two numbers placed at the beginning of a piece of music (The upper number indicates the number of beats in each measure; the lower number indicates which note gets the beat.)
tonic	the first note of a scale
tonic major	a major scale that has the same tonic as a given minor scale (For example, the tonic major of D minor is D major.)
tonic minor	a minor scale that has the same tonic as a given major scale (For example, the tonic minor of G major is G minor.)
transposition	the rewriting of a melody at a different pitch or in a different key
treble clef, G clef	the clef that indicates the location of G on the second line of the staff
triad	a three-note chord
triplet	a group of three notes played in the time of two notes of the same value
whole tone	two semitones; the distance between any two keys with one key (white or black) between them